Ebba Koch · Mughal Architecture

Ebba Koch

Mughal Architecture

An Outline
of Its History and Development
(1526 – 1858)

Prestel

Cover: Agra, view of the Taj Mahall
(Detail from plate XVII).
Frontispiece: Vadodara (Baroda),
tomb of Qutb al-Din Khan,
991/1583.

© **Prestel-Verlag**, Munich 1991
Prestel-Verlag, Mandlstrasse 26, D-8000 München 40,
Federal Republic of Germany
Tel.: (89) 38 17 09 0; Telefax: (89) 38 17 09 35
© Illustrations: Ebba Koch, Vienna

Distributed in continental Europe by Prestel-Verlag
Verlegerdienst München GmbH & Co KG,
Gutenbergstrasse 1, D-8031 Gilching, Federal Republic of Germany
Tel.: (81 05) 21 10; Telefax: (81 05) 55 20

Distributed in the USA and Canada on behalf of Prestel-Verlag
by te Neues Publishing Company,
15 East 76th Street, New York, NY 10021, USA
Tel.: (212) 2 88 02 65; Telefax: (212) 5 70 23 73

Distributed in Japan on behalf of Prestel-Verlag
by YOHAN-Western Publications Distribution Agency,
14-9 Okubo 3-chome, Shinjuku-ku, J-Tokyo 169
Tel.: (3) 2 08 01 81; Telefax: (3) 2 09 02 88

Distributed in the United Kingdom, Ireland and all other countries
on behalf of Prestel-Verlag
by Thames & Hudson Limited, 30–40 Bloomsbury Street,
London WC1B 3QP, England
Tel.: (71) 6 36 54 88; Telefax: (71) 6 36 47 99

CIP-Titelaufnahme der Deutschen Bibliothek

Koch, Ebba:
Mughal architecture : an outline
Ebba Koch. – Munich : Prestel, 1991
ISBN 3-7913-1070-4
NE: HST

Series cover design: KMS-TEAM
Typesetting: Bosch-Druck, 8300 Landshut/Ergolding
Color separations: Karl Dörfel Reproduktionsges. mbH, Munich
Printing and binding: Bosch-Druck, 8300 Landshut/Ergolding

Printed in Germany

ISBN 3-7913-1070-4

To my son Sebastian

La derniere fois que je la vis [the Taj Mahall] fut avec un de nos Marchands François qui ne pouvoit aussi bien que moy se lasser de le regarder; je n'osois luy en dire mon sentiment apprehendant de m'étre corrompu le goust &, me l'étre fait à l'Indienne; mais comme il revenoit fraichement de France, je fus bien aise de luy entendre dire qu'il n'avoit jamais rien veu de si auguste ny de si hardy dans l'Europe.

The last time I saw it [the Taj Mahall] was in the company of one of our French merchants, who, like myself, did not tire of looking at it. I did not dare to express my opinion, fearing that my taste might have become corrupted and Indianized; but since he had recently come from France, it was quite a relief for me to hear him say that he had seen nothing in Europe so grandiose and daring.

François Bernier
Voyages (1699)

The volume here submitted to the public requires more than the usual measure of explanation and apology, in particular for treating such a vast subject in so brief a way. But, like my earlier book *Shah Jahan and Orpheus*, it was an entirely unplanned child.

In spring 1988 I was asked by Professor C. F. Bosworth, one of the editors of the second edition of the *Encyclopaedia of Islam*, to do the article on Mughal architecture. When I set to work I realized that what I had to do was practically to write a new outline of Mughal architecture. Recent research in the field, our better knowledge of Timurid architecture (which has now become more accessible through the publications of Golombek and Wilber and O'Kane), and not least my own ten years of fieldwork in India, Iran and central Asia made me feel that I would not do justice to the subject by repeating once more the conventional opinions. In order to explain just the general trends, many gaps had to be closed at least superficially. That meant that the existing knowledge from the published sources had to be combined with new, unpublished material. This was particularly necessary as regards the "Timurid connection" of Mughal architecture and the main trends in the funerary architecture of Jahangir's reign and in the mosques of Shah Jahan. When I had finished writing it the text had become much longer than originally planned, and only a brief abstract of it was used for the encyclopaedia. After I had tried out the material in a lecture at New Delhi in autumn 1989, friends and colleagues persuaded me to publish it in the form of a book. Their argument was that a ready reference on Mughal architecture was greatly needed, the more so since there has not been any monograph devoted to this subject so far.

The text has been conceived to provide the reader interested in Mughal architecture with concise, up-to-date information about its stylistic development and types of building. I also hope that by the presentation of new material the book will broaden our picture of Mughal architecture, and that by fresh analysis it will stimulate further research and discussion. However, I would not claim that the work lives up to the classical standard of constituting "one harmonious whole". The formative phases of Mughal architecture are treated more fully than the later periods, where even the most basic research is still wanting. Often, preference is given to the tracing of stylistic developments over a rigid classification of building types; the index will compensate for that. Notes are kept to a minimum; they usually refer either to contemporary sources or to the most recent secondary literature. A bibliography for further reading is provided at the end of the book.

The transliteration of Persian and Arabic words follows the system of the *Cambridge History of Islam*, with a few exceptions. Thus, I have employed "ay" for the diphthong "ai" and the Arabic forms "th" and "w" for the Persian "s̱" and "v". Diacritical marks have been confined to the transliteration of technical terms in the glossary and to the citation of contemporary sources in the bibliography. Place-names are rendered in their current form. Names of monuments between quotation marks are those of local tradition not supported by historical evidence. The use of Persian, Arabic and Sanskrit-derived architectural terms follows the practice of the Mughal sources; these terms are explained in the glossary. Every Muslim date of the Hijra era is followed by an oblique and the corresponding Christian date converted according to Freeman-Grenville.

My thanks go to Professor C. E. Bosworth for providing the impulse for me to draw together my ideas on Mughal architecture and for his encouraging first reaction to the result. I am particularly indebted to the Archaeological Survey of India for repeated permission granted over the years to survey the Muslim monuments of India. I profited greatly from stimulating discussions with Dr W. H. Siddiqi and Dr Z. A. Desai. With gratitude I also acknowledge the assistance I have had from the Department of Archaeology and Museums, Government of Pakistan, in particular from Dr Ahmad Nabi Khan, Dr M. Rafique Mughal and Masood ul-Hasan Khokhar. I also thank Dr Saifur Rahman Dar, director of the Lahore Museum. My scale drawings of the forts of Agra, Allahabad and Delhi could not have been made without the generous permission of the Indian Army; my special thanks go to General O. P. Malhotra, General Gauri Shankar and General P. N. Kathpalia. All photography not specifically credited to others were taked by myself; all drawings, unless otherwise indicated, were prepared by the architect Richard A. Barraud from measurements taken by him and myself. I am glad to have the occasion to acknowledge here for the first but certainly not for the last time the professional interest, the great care and the good will he has devoted throughout the years to this aspect of my work. I also thank Glen Scaife for his help with the drawings. My findings are based in many instances on Mughal texts and still unpublished manuscripts, the translation of which I could not have carried out without the assistance of Dr S. M. Yunus Jaffery from Zakir Husain College (formerly Delhi College). I hope that he will be pleased to find in this book a photograph of the historic building in which he works and lives, and where he initiated me into the Persian language. I am indebted to three colleagues for kindly putting unpublished manuscripts at my disposal: Professor Iqtidar Alam Khan from Aligarh Muslim University (Mughal caravanserais and Mughal buildings of Bayana including a plan of Maryam al-Zamani 's *ba'oli*), Professor Annemarie Schimmel (patronage of ᶜAbd al-Rahim Khan-i Khanan) and Dr Catherine B. Asher (patronage of Raja Man Singh). Dr Aśok Kumar Das, Yaduendra Sahai and Dr B. M. Jawalia were most helpful during my research in the Maharaja Sawai Man Singh II Museum in the City Palace of Jaipur. I am further indebted for encouragement, information, stimulating suggestions and help in more practical matters to many friends and colleagues, especially Jürgen Borchhardt, Ikram Chaghtai, Andrew Cooks, Simon Digby, Albertine Gaur, Susan Gole, Narayani Gupta, Jery Losty, George Michell (in particular for his advice in matters of fieldwork), Attilio Petruccioli (for giving me permission to publish one of his plans of Fatehpur Sikri), Brijender, Shashi and Pincha Singh (for hospitality and help in Delhi), Robert Skelton (for hospitality in London), Angela Völker and last but not least Mark Zebrowski for his initial encouragement in 1976 to take up the study of Mughal architecture. During a visit to Vienna in December 1988, Partha and Swasti Mitter read an early draft of the manuscript and made very helpful suggestions to improve its linguistic form.

In Austria I am indebted to the Fonds zur Förderung der wissenschaftlichen Forschung, in particular to Dr Raoul F. Kneucker, for a grant which enabled me to carry out the present work. I also thank Dr Erhard Busek, Minister for Science and Research, for his kind interest and support.

And I am forever beholden to my husband Benno for his willingness at all times to share me with the Mughals.

Vienna, October 1990   F. K.

Introduction

The architecture of southern Asia owes to the patronage of the Mughals one of its most creative and richest periods. Each of the Muslim dynasties that established themselves in the Indian subcontinent from the end of the twelfth century onwards created its own architectural style, but no other period of Indo-Islamic architecture before the Mughals has bequeathed to us such a wealth of outstanding secular and religious buildings.

But before we concentrate on purely architectural issues it will be helpful to provide the reader new to the subject with a little general information on the Mughals.[1] Those already familiar with the Mughals will perhaps prefer to proceed to the second part of the introduction.

I The Mughals

In Arabic and Persian, *mughal* means "the Mongol" or "Mongolian", because Babur, the founder of the Indian Mughal dynasty, was descended on his mother's side from Chingiz Khan. More important for the self-understanding of the Mughals, however, was Babur's paternal descent from Timur, the great Asian conqueror of the later fourteenth and early fifteenth century. With this Timurid-Mongolian heritage, the Mughals withstood Indianization, at least with regard to physiognomy and language, until about 1600. Up to this time family portraits still show Tartarian features, and Chaghatay Turki was spoken in the family. By and by, through dynastic marriages with Rajput princesses, the Mughals became more Indianized. Also, the family Turki gave way to Persian, which was already the official language of the court, of the administration and, of course, of poetry.

Babur's impressive progress through life as general and emperor (*padshah*) was still marked by the Mongolian drive to conquer, in his case however softened by a truly humanistic approach towards life. He began his career as ruler of a small Timurid principality in the central Asian region of Ferghana. After his attempt to establish himself as ruler of Samarqand failed, Babur took another cue from his great ancestor Timur − who had invaded Delhi in 801/1398 − and turned his attention southwards to India. He occupied Kabul and from there, in the famous battle of Panipat (932/1526), defeated the Lodi sultan of Delhi, who then ruled over northern India. Initially, Babur was all but pleased with his new conquest: in his rightly famous memoirs, the *Babur nama*, he criticizes the heat, the dust, the mentality, the art, the architecture and the fruits of Hindustan. He died after only four years of rule in India, and was buried in Kabul.

Babur left to his son and successor Humayun ("the August") a territory still to be consolidated. The second Mughal almost lost again what had been conquered of Hindustan to his local rival, the Afghan chief of Bihar, Shir Shah Suri. After several devastating defeats, Humayun had to take refuge at the court of Shah Tahmasp I of Persia (r. 1524−76). With his help he reconquered northern India in 1555 but died soon after, in 1556, from a fall on the stairs of his library at Delhi. During Humayun's absence the highly capable

[1] The introductory remarks on the Mughal dynasty are based on the project-study for an exhibition on "The Mughals and Europe", planned by Joachim Deppert and myself. A good overview on the Mughals is given by M. G. S. Hodgson; easier reading illustrated with photographs is provided by Gascoigne − the work has also been translated into German.

Shir Shah had laid the basis for the administration and organization of an imperial state, spadework from which the Mughals were to profit.

Akbar, the son of Humayun, was enthroned at the age of fourteen and ruled until 1605 (pl. I). Called rightly "the Great" (*akbar*), he became the most important ruler of the Mughal dynasty. With the support of highly capable nobles, in particular his friend the liberal thinker and author Abu'l Fazl ᶜAllami, Akbar expanded the empire over the greater part of India. He brought Malwa, the Rajput states, Gujarat, Bengal, Kashmir and Khandesh under Mughal rule and secured the northwest frontier by recapturing Kabul and Qandahar. The latter was however to remain a bone of contention between the Mughals and the Safawid rulers of Persia. Akbar provided India with a modernized military, fiscal and commercial system and a well-functioning administration based on officials of a military aristocracy comprising Turks, Afghans, Persians and Hindus. Nobility was not inherited but acquired through military rank (*mansab*); even the succession to the throne was not regulated by primogeniture. All the land in the hands of the nobility belonged to the crown, and reverted to it after the transfer or the death of the temporary landholders (*jagirdars*). This regulation had a certain dampening effect on non-imperial architectural patronage. Akbar strove for a reconciliation of his Muslim and Hindu subjects, in particular in the intellectual and religious spheres. He had outstanding works of Sanskrit literature translated into Persian and propagated an enlightened religiosity based on reason. His deep intellectual curiosity about religions in general also led him to invite Jesuit missionaries to the Mughal court. On the diplomatic level Akbar had contacts with the Safawids, Özbegs (Uzbeks) and Ottomans, and even planned to send an envoy to the pope and to King Philip II of Spain.

The consolidation under Akbar provided the basis for the flourishing of the Mughal empire during the rule of Akbar's son Jahangir and his grandson Shah Jahan (pl. I). Jahangir ("the World-Seizer", r. 1605–27) continued more or less on the lines of Akbar. In the last phase of his reign the real power was in the hands of his Persian wife Nur Jahan ("Light of the World") and her family – her father, Ghiyath Beg Tehrani (entitled Iᶜtimad al-Daula), who held as *wazir* and *wakil* the highest charges of the empire, and her brother Abu'l Hasan Asaf Khan. Asaf Khan's daughter, Arjumand Banu Begam, was married to Jahangir's son Prince Khurram, the later Shah Jahan, and, as Mumtaz Mahall ("the Chosen One of the Palace"), became famous for the mausoleum he built for her.

Shah Jahan ("the World Ruler", r. 1628–58) was only able to succeed to the throne through the ruthless machinations of Asaf Khan. For the first time other pretenders to the throne were eliminated through murder – the Mughals had lost the moral standards of their first hour. The most prominent victim of Shah Jahan's ambition was his elder brother Khusrau. The deed was excused by Shah Jahan's historian Kanbo as a rightful means to secure the succession and to save the country from turmoil. The Mughal empire did indeed experience its phase of greatest prosperity and stability under the rule of Shah Jahan. His ambition to extend Mughal power further north to Balkh and Badakhshan, however, ended in failure. Shah Jahan's later reign was already overshadowed by the first signs of decline. After an illness of the emperor, his son Aurangzib usurped power in 1658 and waged a savage war for the succession. The struggle culminated in the public execution under the pretext of heresy of his brother Dara Shukoh ("the Glory of Darius"), the favourite son and designated successor of Shah Jahan. Shah Jahan was imprisoned for the rest of his life in the fort of Agra, his daughter Jahanara ("World-Adornment") keeping him company. Entitled Shah Begam, she had enjoyed the status of the first lady of the realm after the death of her mother, Mumtaz Mahall.

Aurangzib ("Throne-Ornament", r. 1658–1707) was, on the one hand, a capable general: he subjugated the Deccani sultanates in the south and thus brought about the greatest expansion of the Mughal empire. On the other hand, he was a strictly orthodox Muslim and broke with the liberal traditions of his predecessors. This stance, together with a loosening grip on the administration, was not conducive to reconciling the heterogeneous tendencies in the empire.

Under Aurangzib's weak successors the Mughal empire soon became debilitated. During the whole of the eighteenth century northern India was at the mercy of indigenous and foreign powers. The English extended their sway from Bengal westwards until they occupied Delhi in 1803. The last two Mughal rulers, Shah Akbar II and Bahadur Shah II, were allowed to rule at least nominally until 1858, when the English took the Great Indian Mutiny as a pretext to depose and exile the last Mughal.

From Babur to Aurangzib the Mughal dynasty produced, in uninterrupted succession, six generations of world-ranking rulers. They combine political and military genius with scientific, artistic, even mystical qualifications of the highest order. The Mughals are not only founders of cities (Akbar, Jahangir, Shah Jahan), architects (Shah Jahan), recognized naturalists and horticulturalists (Jahangir), polo-players (Akbar, Jahangir) and excellent shots (including Jahangir's wife Nur Jahan), but also authors of highly readable autobiographies (Babur, Jahangir), letters (Aurangzib) and poems (Babur); they are calligraphers, collectors of art, sponsors of painting and literature, astronomers (Humayun), religious innovators (Akbar) and authors of philosophical treatises and of mystic works (Dara Shukoh, Jahanara). Their objective and broad-minded disposition – at least up to Shah Jahan, who became more orthodox – also marks their attitude towards religion within the framework of Sunni Islam.

Their brilliant abilities qualified the Mughals particularly well to stand as absolute sovereigns at the head of a centralized state and to give some credence to their propagated ideal of kingship, which was shaped on Muslim caliphal, Qur'anic prophetic, ancient Iranian, Hindu, Sufi and even biblical eschatological models. The descendants of Timur – at least Akbar, Jahangir and Shah Jahan – saw themselves as representatives of God on earth who united both spiritual and political authority. They also prided themselves on being second Solomons or perfect replicas of the prophet-king of Qur'anic sanction. From Humayun to Shah Jahan, the Mughals surrounded themselves with the aura of the mythical and ancient historical kings of Iran and India, and claimed that their wise and just rule would bring to the world of humans and animals a golden age of peace. The Mughals tried earnestly to live up to this image, and architecture, art, poetry, historiography and court life all served to manifest the imperial ideal.

The dominant focus of culture was the court, whose activities were regulated by an etiquette which under Shah Jahan became increasingly more rigid. The court alternated between the metropolises of the empire, Agra, Lahore and Delhi. Delhi eventually became the permanent seat, after Shah Jahan had built a new capital there in 1639–48. The favourite summer residence of the Mughals was at all times the valley of Kashmir.

All in all, the Mughals represent the Indian variant of absolutism, a concept of rulership that determined their patronage of architecture.

II Mughal Architecture

As a new dynasty which felt a strong need to assert its status and as an elitarian minority ruling over a vast territory of peoples of a different creed and culture, the Mughals were highly aware of the potential of architecture as a means of self-representation. A ruler, according to Mughal political thinking, was best represented by his buildings, and kings should therefore erect great buildings as memorials to their fame. Akbar's historian Qandahari writes: "A good name for kings is [achieved by means] of lofty buildings . . . that is to say, the standard of the measure of men is assessed by the worth of [their] building and from their high-mindedness is estimated the state of their house."[2]

And Shah Jahan's (self-appointed) historian Kanbo legitimates his emperor's passion for building as a necessity of good rule: "It is evident that an increase in such things [i. e. buildings and external show] creates esteem for the rulers in the eyes [of the people] and augments respect [for the rulers] and [their own] dignity in the [people's] hearts. In this way the execution of divine injunctions and prohibitions and the enforcement of divine decrees and laws which are the ultimate aim of rulership and kingship are carried out more effectively."[3]

The logical corollary was to represent the emperor also as the cause of stylistic changes in Mughal architecture. At least up to Aurangzib's reign, the official Mughal histories take care to convey the impression that the formative phases of Mughal architecture were determined not by individual architects but by the committed patronage and informed judgment of each emperor. In particular, the court historians of Jahangir and Shah Jahan represent the emperor's taste as the main criterion by which the value of architecture was measured. Unlike Mughal painters, who often signed their works, architects (*mi'maran*) are only rarely mentioned. The men who supervised the actual construction are named more often, but the exact nature of their role in the building process is not defined and remains to be established. As elsewhere in the Islamic world, the building is in the first instance associated with its patron. The fact that architectural innovations usually appear first in buildings sponsored by the emperor (or his closest entourage) testifies to the crucial role the imperial patrons played in the evolution of this art. Since the architecture of each reign possesses such a distinct "physiognomy", it is

[2] Qandahari, pp. 144 f., cf. p. 147; Eng. trans. in Brand and Lowry 1985, pp. 290–91, 294.

[3] Kanbo, iii, p. 18; Eng. trans. after Koch 1982b, p. 259.

legitimate to designate it by the name of the ruling emperor. However, this periodization has no sharp dividing lines, and transition from one period to the next is smooth.

From the very beginning the emperor's patronship was echoed by nobles of the court and by Mughal officials in the expanding empire; these had a definite share in shaping the image of Mughal architecture, which thus had an ever broadening base in terms of buildings and patrons.

Mughal architecture created a supremely confident style by synthesizing the most heterogeneous elements: Transoxanian,[4] Timurid, Indian, Persian and European. The supraregional character of Mughal architecture sets it apart from the earlier Islamic architecture of the Indian subcontinent and gives it a universal appeal. At the same time, Mughal architecture was not strictly dogmatic, and remained flexible towards regional conditions and building traditions.

Since the Mughals were direct heirs to the Timurids, the sustaining element of their architecture, especially during the initial phase, was Timurid (in the older literature often considered to be "Persian"). A fact that is not generally recognized is that essential ideas of Timurid architecture, such as the perfect symmetry of plan reflected consistently in the elevations, as well as complex vault patterns, came to fruition much more in Mughal architecture than in Safawid Iran, which was also heir to the same tradition.[5]

[4] I have used Transoxania for those parts of central Asia described by the Mughals as *Ma wara' al-nahr*, "the land which lies beyond the river", roughly the area between Oxus (Amu Darya) and Jaxartes (Syr Darya).

[5] Pougatchenkova, p. 62.

Map of central and southern Asia with places mentioned in the text.

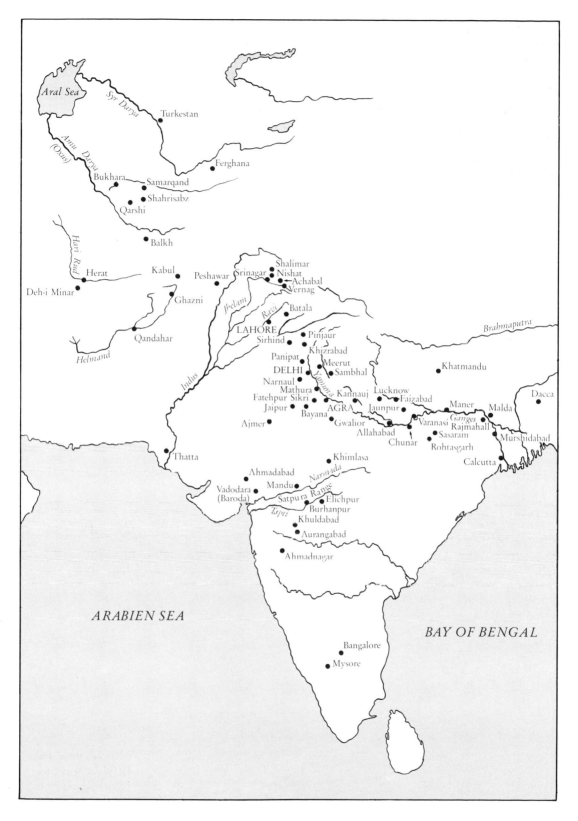

Aral Sea

Syr Darya

Turkestan

Amu Darya
(Oxus)

Ferghana

Bukhara
Samarqand
Shahrisabz
Qarshi

Balkh

Hari Rud

Herat
Kabul
Peshawar
Srinagar
Shalimar
Nishat
Achabal
Vernag

Deh-i Minar

Ghazni

Jhelam

Batala

Ravi

Qandahar

LAHORE
Sirhind
Pinjaur

Helmand

Khizrabad

Panipat
Meerut
Khatmandu

Brahmaputra

Indus

DELHI
Sambhal

Narnaul
Mathura
Kannauj
Lucknow
Dacca

Fatehpur Sikri
Yamuna
Faizabad
Maner
Malda

Jaipur
Bayana
AGRA
Jaunpur
Ganges

Ajmer
Gwalior
Varanasi
Rajmahall

Allahabad
Sasaram
Murshidabad

Chunar
Rohtasgarh

Thatta
Khimlasa

Calcutta

Ahmadabad
Narmada

Vadodara
(Baroda)
Mandu
Elichpur

Satpura Range
Burhanpur

Tapti
Khuldabad

Aurangabad

Ahmadnagar

ARABIEN SEA

BAY OF BENGAL

Bangalore
Mysore

I   Bichitr, dynastic group portrait: Akbar seated between his son Jahangir and his grandson Shah Jahan transfers the Timurid crown to the latter. Before each ruler stands his wazir: from left to right, I'timad al-Daula, Khan-i A'zam, Asaf Khan. From the Minto album, Mughal, 1630–31. Gouache, 29.7 x 20.5 cm. Reproduced by courtesy of the Trustees of the Chester Beatty Library, Dublin, MS 7, no. 19. (Photo: R. Skelton)

II Delhi, Quwwat al-Islam Masjid, Ala'i Darwaza, 710/1311. At left part of the
Qutb Minar, end of the twelfth to thirteenth centuries.
(Photo 1979)

III   Delhi, tomb of Humayun, 1562–71. (Photo 1989)

*IV   Agra fort, Jahangiri Mahall, later 1560s–1570s,
west (landward) facade. (Photo 1986)*

V   Fatehpur Sikri, Jamiͨ Masjid, c. 1568–78,
Buland Darwaza, outer facade. (Photo 1978)

VI   Vrindavan, temple of Madan Mohan,
built in the style of Fatehpur Sikri. (Photo 1978)

IX *Agra, Sikandra, tomb of Akbar, 1022/1613,*
seen from one of the minarets of the southern gate.
(Photo 1978)

VII *Agra, Sikandra, tomb of Akbar,*
1022/1613, vestibule of corridor leading to
tomb-chamber. (Photo 1977)

VIII *Lahore fort, Kala Burj, early 17th century,*
vault painted with angels and birds. (Photo 1980)

X Ajmer, Chashma-i Nur, completed 1024/1615.
(Photo 1982)

*XI Shaikhupura near Lahore, hunting-palace,
1607–20, restored 1634–35. (Photo 1979)*

*XIV Agra, Taj Mahall complex, tomb attributed to Fatehpuri Begam,
1640s–1650s. At right, the enclosure wall of the tomb garden,
the domes of the mosque, of a pavilion, and of the mausoleum. (Photo 1978)*

*XII Delhi, Shahjahanabad, Jami^c Masjid, 1060–66/1650–56.
(Photo 1978)*

*XIII Agra fort, eastern front. From left to right, the Jahangiri Mahall,
the Bangla-i Jahanara, the Aramgah, the Bangla-i Darshan,
and the Shah Burj. (Photo 1979)*

XV   Shalimar gardens of Lahore, 1641–42.
Painting, 12 x 46 cm. Sikh period (1767–1846).
Lahore Museum. (Photo 1980)

XVI   Delhi, Red Fort, Diwan-i ʿAmm, Florentine pietre dure panels
showing Orpheus playing to the beasts, birds and flowers,
with interspersed Mughal work depicting Indian birds
(kingfishers and parakeets) on the wall behind the throne-jharoka. (Photo 1981)

*XVII Agra, view of the Taj Mahall seen from the Red Fort
across the Jamna, 1041–52/1632–43. (Photo 1980)*

XVIII   Aurangabad, tomb of Rabiʿa Daurani, 1071/1660–61. (Photo 1982)

*XIX   Aurangabad, tomb of Rabiʿa Daurani,
detail of ornamented door.
(Photo 1982)*

*XX   Lahore, Badshahi Masjid, 1084/1673–74.
(Photo 1980)*

*XXI   Delhi, tomb of Safdar Jang, 1167/1753–54.
(Photo 1986)*

The initial phase of Mughal architecture under Babur is difficult to evaluate because of the discrepancy between his own writing about architecture, which sets high Timurid standards, and the few buildings that have survived.[1] Although he is celebrated as a founder of gardens, it is his mosques in Sambhal (933/1526), Ayodhya and Panipat (both 935/1528–29) that remain as chief monuments from his brief reign. They attempt to do justice to a large scale by borrowing inadequate forms of the decaying Sultanate architecture. The Panipat mosque, however, shows an important innovative feature in the form of Timurid arch-netted transition zones in pseudostructural plaster relief-work applied to the pendentives of the small domes of the

1 Panipat, Kabuli Bagh Masjid, south wing of the prayer-hall, ruined bay with arch-netted pendentives in pseudostructural plaster relief-work. (Photo 1982)

lateral bays.[2] This system of intersecting arched ribs weaving the pendentives (or in larger domes the apexes of the squinches and blind wall-arches) of the transition zone into a continous zigzag baseline for the dome (or vault) was to become Mughal standard (figs. 21, 85) (the actual brick or stone construction behind this plaster or sandstone shell was usually corbelled). It was a suppler and more elegant solution than that of north Indian Sultanate architecture, where the transition to the baseline of the dome was effected by corbelled registers of blind arcades and multi-sided bands. This system was still employed for the main dome over the *mihrab* chamber of the Panipat mosque. For the construction of large domes the Sultanate scheme persisted – alongside the new arch-netting – well into Akbar's reign (fig. 58); and in non-imperial buildings even into later periods.

Of Babur's gardens in India, the rock-cut Bagh-i Nilufar ("Lotus-Garden") at Dholpur (933–35/1527–29) south of Agra is preserved to some extent.[3] Its modest structures are however in somewhat disappointing contrast to what

[1] For a recent survey of Babur's buildings see Crane.

[2] For this specific form of Timurid vaulting see most recently O'Kane, pp. 51 ff. et passim; Golombek and Wilber, pp. 107 ff. et passim, with further literature.

[3] Moynihan 1988.

[4] Eng. trans. pp. 606 f., 634.

[5] Singh, pp. 190 f.; Gole 1989, pls. 114, 114a.

one would have expected from Babur's description in his memoirs, the *Babur nama*.[4] Only fragments remain of his famous Chahar (Char) Bagh ("Fourfold Garden") or Bagh-i Hasht Bihisht ("Garden of the Eight Paradises") at Agra. According to a recently discovered eighteenth-century plan of Agra in the Jaipur Palace Museum,[5] on which it features – inscribed in *devanagari* script – as "*chahar bag patishahi*" [*chahar bagh padshahi*] next to a "*chahar bag dusarau patishahi*" ("second imperial fourfold garden"), the garden was situated on the other side of the river Jamna (Yamuna) adjoining the Mahtab Bagh and almost opposite the later Taj Mahall. It introduced into India the

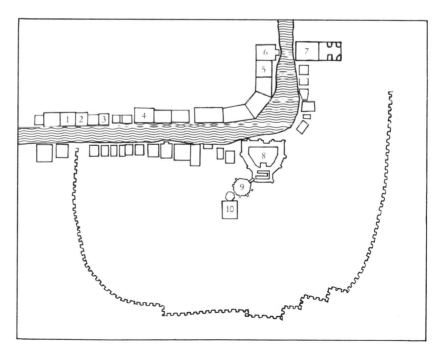

Timurid-Persian scheme of a walled-in garden subdivided (ideally, but not necessarily, into four quarters) by raised walkways (*khiyaban*) and canals (*nahr*), and became the "foundation-stone" for the development of Mughal Agra as a "riverbank" city with a bandlike succession of walled gardens on both sides of the Jamna. According to Babur's companion Zayn Khan,[6] Babur's nobles followed his example by building gardens "on the models of Khurasani edifices".[7] Other indispensable amenities of Timurid lifestyle, such as "four royal hot-baths", were constructed "in the cities of Hindustan" to please the "Khurasanis and Samarqandis" who had come with Babur to India.[8]

When Babur died in 1530 he was not entombed in India, which shows that the Mughals did not yet feel quite at home in their new territories. Babur's body was brought to Kabul and buried under a simple marble tombstone in one of the gardens of that city.[9]

[6] Eng. trans. pp. 160 f.

[7] At the time of the Mughals the term Khurasan had a much wider connotation than today, also covering parts of what are now Soviet central Asia and Afghanistan. See O'Kane, pp. 1 ff.

[8] See note 6.

[9] Bogdanov.

A heterogeneous picture of Mughal architecture prevails during the next period, the two phases of Humayun's reign up to the middle of the sixteenth century. The Timurid strand is represented by almost pure imports such as the mosque at Kachpura, Agra (937/1530–31).[1] But for the missing outer dome, the building shares its main features with the sixteenth-century Namazgah mosque at Qarshi, a town southwest of Samarqand mentioned by

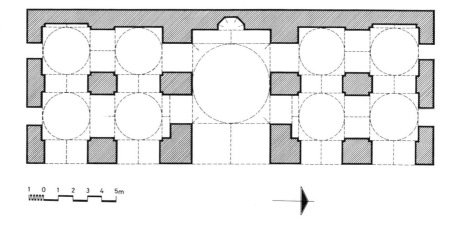

4 Agra, Kachpura mosque, reconstructed ground-plan.

5 Agra, Kachpura mosque, 937/1530–31. (Photo 1978)

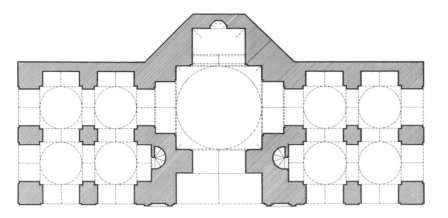

6 Qarshi, Namazgah mosque, 16th century, ground-plan. (After Yaralova et al.).

Babur in his memoirs.[2] These features are a central domed chamber preceded by a high *pishtaq* (portal in form of a monumental arched niche in a rectangular frame), and flanked by lower lateral wings (open on three sides) of four domed bays demarcated by masonry piers. All domes show the characteristic arch-netting in the transition zones.

Two anonymous tombs at Delhi fall into the same category of Timurid-derived imports and, on stylistic grounds, can safely be dated to this period. These mausoleums, now known as the "Sabz Burj" ("Green Tower") and the "Nila Gumbad" ("Blue Dome"),[3] introduce to northern India a late-Timurid formula for octagonal tombs. The common features of the two buildings are their elegant proportions – more pronounced in the Sabz Burj, which reflects late-Timurid ideals with its elongated *pishtaq*s and a

7 Delhi, Sabz Burj, 1530s–1540s. (Photo 1976, before restoration)

36

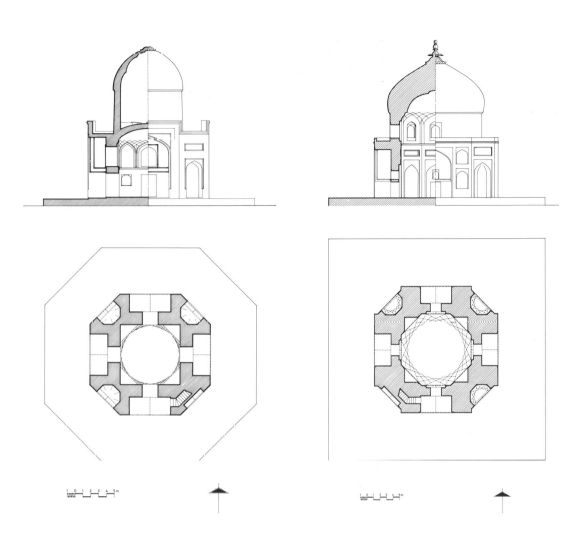

8 *Delhi, Sabz Burj,
ground-plan,
half-section and
half-elevation.*

9 *Delhi, Nila
Gumbad, 1530s–1540s,
ground-plan,
half-section and
half-elevation.*

slightly bulbous dome set on a high cylindical drum housing an inner lower
dome – their four-centred arches, their outer facing with tile-work arranged
in geometrical patterns and the painted plaster decoration and arch-netting
of their vaults. The ground-plan of this tomb type is in the form of an irregular octagon. It contains a central square (cruciform) chamber connected to
axial *pishtaq*s in the outer faces, which alternate with smaller (half-octagonal)
niches in the narrower sides. This plan follows a late- and post-Timurid form
that had appeared in the shrine of Momo Sharifan at Ghazni (c. 1500)[4] or
in the funerary mosque of Abu Nasr Parsa at Balkh[5] (here only one *pishtaq*
connects with the inner domed chamber). To describe the plan – as
Golombek and Wilbur do – as an octagonal version of a cross-in-square
plan is to define it in its widest sense. In the Timurid context I would pro-
pose reading the plan as an abbreviation of the ninefold plan, also called
hasht bihisht. Combined with Mughalized elevations, this plan became a
standard formula for small mausoleums and garden pavilions.[6]

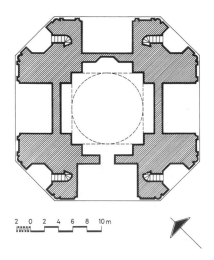

2 0 2 4 6 8 10 m

10 *Balkh, mosque of Abu Nasr Parsa, dated variously to c. 1460 and to the later 16th century, ground-plan.*

The Timurid element was soon to merge with local building traditions, in particular with regard to the facing of buildings and architectural decoration. The main source of inspiration here was the revival of the ornamental sandstone style of the early Delhi Sultanate (pl. II). It had gone out of fashion during the fourteenth and fifteenth centuries in Delhi but continued uninterrupted in provincial centres (Bayana, Kannauj), creating an architectural heritage from which early Mughal and Suri architecture could draw their inspiration.[7] Characteristic of this style is a highly ornate revetment of buildings with red or buff sandstone, inlays of white marble and other coloured stone, wall surfaces covered with flat geometrical ornaments, carved motifs such as budfringed arches (often read as spearheads), lotus rosettes, engaged corner shafts or colonnettes, coffered pilasters, perforated stone screens (*jalis*), ribbed domes or domes with a lotus pattern, wide *chhajja* eaves, and monolithic sandstone pillars and stepped ornamental brackets in trabeate constructions. Typical examples are the buildings of the Purana Qilᶜa ("Old Fort") at Delhi – the palace-citadel founded in 939/1533 as Dinpanah ("Asylum of the Faith") by Humayun and subsequently altered by Shir Shah Suri and probably also by Akbar – particularly the mosque, which, on the basis of literary evidence, must however be attributed to Shir Shah (early 1540s).[8] The characteristic decorative treatment is applied to a massive single-aisle mosque with five vaulted bays (of which the end bays are narrower) and an outer central dome, a building type rooted in the local Delhi tradition (Moth ki Masjid, c. 911/1505, Jamali Kamali Masjid at Mehrauli, first third of sixteenth century).

The only surviving palace building in the citadel, the two-storey octagonal "Sher Mandal" ("Shir [Shah]'s Pavilion"), represents a Timurid-Safawid pavilion type. The cruciform interior of the upper storey is connected by axial passages to four of the outer eight niches, which are linked in turn so as to form an ambulatory.[9] The inner dome and the arch-netting of the vaults is also of Timurid inspiration. The pattern lining the four half-vaults

[7] Koch 1987a, p. 135 f.

[8] Asher 1981; for plans of the citadel and the mosque see Joshi, figs. 1, 2.

[9] For a plan see Petruccioli 1988, fig. 237.

[10] See below, p. 48.

38

11 *Delhi, Purana Qil'a, Sher Mandal, probably second half of 16th century. (Photo 1982)*

of the cruciform chamber has a close relative in the curvilinear netted diaper pattern of the half-vaults of the tomb of Qutb al-Din Muhammad Khan (991/1583) at Vadodara (Baroda).[10] This may serve as an indication for the true date of the Sher Mandal, which – despite its popular name – is usually described as the library of Humayun where he fell to his death. The structure is clad in the local red sandstone and crowned with a *chhatri* (small domed kiosk), a typical feature of Indian (Sultanate) architecture that was

12 *Bayana, Vijayamandirgarh fort, pavilion of Muhammad, 940/1533–34. (Photo 1984)*

13 Isfahan, ʿAli
Qapu, 17th century.
(Photo 1978)

14 Bukhara, Balyand
mosque, first half of
the 16th century,
pillared timber porch
(columns remodelled
after the originals).
(Photo 1981)

15 *Khimlasa fort,*
Nagina Mahall,
probably 15th century.
(Photo 1983)

16 *Fatehpur Sikri,*
Panch Mahall, 1570s.
(Photo 1978)

[11] Andrews 1986b.

[12] The inscription
was discovered by
I. A. Khan 1990, who
also gives plans of
the two storeys; cf.
Jahangir, Eng. trans.
ii, p. 63.

readily adopted by the Mughals. Such confident synthesizing will be more
typical of Akbar's architecture.

None of Humayun's own palace buildings described by his author Khwandamir seems to have survived.[11] The first preserved Mughal residential
building that can be dated is the recently identified pavilion of Muhammad,
Humayun's *bakhshi*, near the tomb of Shaykh Bahlul in the fort of Vijayamandirgarh, Bayana. According to the chronogram of its inscription it
was built in 940/1533–34.[12] The small stepped pavilion of red sandstone,
which appears rather modest at first glance, is nevertheless a key building of
Mughal palace architecture. It evidences two paradigmatic constituent

elements: the flat-roofed post-and-beam construction and, on the main floor, the configuration of a closed central block with a verandah running round it. This connects it not only to a long local tradition of trabeate pillared halls, but also to masonry buildings with post-and-beam (timber) porches in Iran and Transoxania. In Iran the pillared hall was called *talar* and in Transoxania *iwan*. The use of the term *iwan* to designate pillared constructions was adopted by the Mughals, which attests to their interest in the post-and-beam architecture of the land of their ancestors.[13] As a variant of the stepped superimposed trabeate constructions, the Bayana pavilion forms a link between pre-Mughal Indo-Islamic forerunners such as the "Nagina Mahall" ("Jewel Palace") in the fort of Khimlasa in Madhya Pradesh (probably fifteenth century)[14] and the striking "Panch Mahall" ("Five [-storeyed] Palace") at Fatehpur Sikri of Akbar's time. Significantly, Akbar's historian Qandahari seems to refer to the Panch Mahall as "*iwan khana*", or "pillared house".[15]

From Akbar's period onwards this building type is also adapted to an octagonal plan. It appears as independent pavilion in the one-storey "Qush Khana" ("Falconry") near the Ajmeri Darwaza at Fatehpur Sikri (probably 1570s). The stepped variant is employed for the upper, residential part of towers in a fortificatory or garden context ("Chalis Sutun" ["Forty-pillared Hall"], Allahabad fort, 1583 [fig. 55]; Shah Jahan's Shah Burj in the Agra fort, completed 1637 [pl. XIII]).

[13] Koch 1982a, p. 331, n. 4; 1987a, p. 139.

[14] Koch 1987a, pp. 131–33.

[15] p. 151.

Mughal architecture attained its distinctive character during the reign of Akbar, whose syncretistic genius had its impact not only on the political affairs of the Mughal empire but also on the development of the arts. Military conquests were reflected in architecture, a process helped by an influx of craftsmen from the new provinces to the Mughal court. Akbar's architectural activity surpassed even that of the Tughluqs,[1] who had already shown a mania for building. Akbari architecture developed into a dramatic supraregional synthesis characterized by extensive borrowing of features from earlier Timurid, Transoxanian, Indian and Persian styles. Stylistic clashes resulting from the amalgamation of such heterogeneous elements were mollified by the favourite building material, red sandstone, whose unifying hue carried an additional attraction in being the colour reserved for imperial tents.

In the uninhibited interaction of styles, however, there was a certain predilection for particular types of building. The Timurid tradition made itself most felt in vaulted masonry architecture employed for mausoleums, individual palace buildings (pleasure-kiosks), gatehouses (often serving residential purposes), *hammams*, *karwansara'i*s and smaller mosques.

Funerary and secular architecture and the Timurid ninefold plan (*hasht bihisht*)

With the first major building enterprise of Akbar's period, the tomb of his father at Delhi, Mughal architecture came into its own (pl. III). The tomb of Humayun is a synthesis of creatively developed Timurid ideas and local traditions, the whole breathing true Mughal splendour in its perfect planning. It is the first of the grand dynastic mausoleums that were to become synonyms of Mughal architecture. Here for the first time the monumental scale is attained that was to be characteristic of imperial projects. It is one

18   Delhi, tomb of Humayun, sectional elevation.

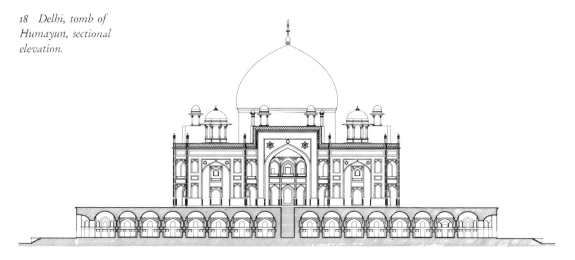

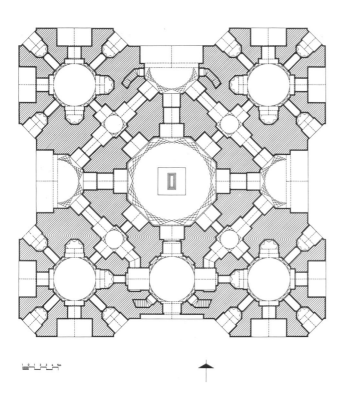

19   Delhi, tomb of
Humayun,
ground-plan.

of the few buildings of the period that can be connected with named architects, namely Sayyid Muhammad and his father, Mirak Sayyid Ghiyath. According to a sixteenth-century source traced by Simon Digby, both were architects (and poets!) of distinction, working for Husayn Bayqara in the late-Timurid capital Herat, Babur in India and, during Humayun's exile, the Özbeg (Uzbek) ruler in Bukhara. After the Mughal restoration, the son returned to India and was entrusted with the construction of Humayun's tomb between 970 and 978/1562 and 1571.[2] The role that Humayun's widow Hajji Begam (d. 1582) played in the construction of the tomb has been overemphasized by past scholarship. According to Abu'l Fazl, the main chronicler of Akbar's reign, she merely took charge of the maintenance of the mausoleum during the last two years of her life.[3]

The mausoleum is situated in the centre of the first preserved Mughal garden on a classical *char bagh* pattern. The *khiyaban*s (paved walkways) that divide the garden into its four parts terminate in gatehouses and subsidiary structures.[4] The tomb is clad in red sandstone highlighted with white marble. The slightly bulbous dome is faced entirely with white marble. The studied handling of the two colours puts into relief each element of the elevation, and thus consummates a tradition of the earlier Sultanate architecture of Delhi best represented by Sultan ʿAlaʾ al-Din Khalji's ʿAlaʾi Darwaza (710/1311; pl. II). The intricate ground-plan of the main body of Humayun's tomb, which stands on a large podium housing 124 vaulted chambers, ingeniously elaborates on a scheme that was to be much used in Mughal architecture, the already mentioned ninefold plan or *hasht bihisht*.[5]

[1] Turkish dynasty with its seat at Delhi, ruling over large parts of India during the fourteenth century.

[2] Bukhari, pp. 37–38, 103, 283–86; Eng. intro. pp. 23–24. Personal communication of S. Digby in a letter of 18.5.1989. Bada'uni, Eng. trans. ii, p. 135, names only Mirak Mirza Ghiyath as the builder of the tomb.

[3] Abu'l Fazl, *Akbar nama*, Eng. trans. iii, p. 551.

The Mughals derived this concept from its late (or post-) Timurid versions: the abbreviated form had already appeared in the Sabz Burj and the Nila Gumbad. A fuller form had been employed in the *khanaqah* of Shaykh Armani in Deh-i Minar southwest of Herat (late fifteenth century)[6] and in the still more complex *khanaqah* of Qasim Shaykh at Kermin, northeast of Bukhara (1558–59).[7]

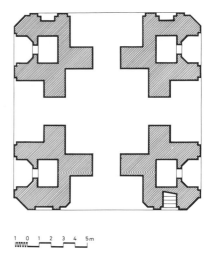

20 *Deh-i Minar near Herat, khanaqa of Shaykh Armani, later 15th century, ground-plan.*

The complete ninefold plan – as it became current in Mughal architecture – consists of a square (or rectangle), sometimes with corners fortified by towers but more often chamfered so as to form an irregular octagon (termed *muthamman baghdadi* by the Mughals). The layout is divided by four intersecting construction lines into nine parts, comprising a domed chamber in the centre, rectangular open halls in the middle of the sides – in the form either of *pishtaq*s or of flat-roofed verandahs supported by pillars (the Mughal *iwan*) – and two-storey vaulted rooms or blocks in the corners, reflected on the facade by superimposed vaulted niches (*nashiman*) (figs. 54, 153). In the radially planned versions of this scheme the corner rooms are linked to the main domed chamber by additional diagonal passages (figs. 24, 108). The term *hasht bihisht* ("eight paradises") has been interpreted as a reference to the eight rooms surrounding the central chamber.[8] While in preserved Timurid architecture buildings with such a strictly symmetrical ninefold plan represent the exception rather than the rule, it is the characteristic contribution of Mughal architecture to have adopted and further developed the model in a perfect symmetry faithfully reflected in the elevation.

The plan of Humayun's tomb is composed of four such irregular octagonal units, which in turn form the corner elements of the main nine-part figure. This clear and yet complex scheme of overlapping points of reference – which uses the typical to produce the outstanding – makes the structure one of the most perfectly planned octagonal buildings in the general history of architecture. The design appears to have been inspired by Humayun's wooden boat palace, which is known to us only through its description by

[4] For an overall plan and description see Naqvi; for the most recent discussion see Lowry, with further literature.

[5] Jairazbhoy 1961; Hoag 1968; Golombek 1981.

[6] For a description of this monument see Golombek and Wilber, i, cat. no. 64; O'Kane, cat. no. 34.

[7] Golombek 1981, pl. 16.

[8] Jairazbhoy 1958, p. 72.

Khwandamir.[9] The floating structure was made of four two-storey pavilions (*chahar taq*) on boats so joined together that between each of the four an arched unit (*taq*) was produced. The eight *hasht bihisht* units − Khwandamir uses the synonym *hasht jannat* − formed on octagonal pool between them. The description also fits the tomb in all its main features, with the exception of the inner pool that takes the place of the octagonal domed hall in the centre.

21 *Delhi, tomb of Humayun, central dome. (Photo 1980)*

We here encounter a phenomenon that was to become a characteristic feature of Mughal architecture. Ideas of funerary and residential architecture were almost entirely interchangeable. In Akbar's period the ninefold plan became the ground-plan par excellence. It was used with imaginative variations in residential and funerary architecture. It was particularly popular for individual palace buildings (Akbar's pavilion in the fort of Ajmer, 978/1570, with a flat ceiling in the central hall[10]) and pleasure-houses in the context of garden or water architecture ("Todar Mal's Baradari", Fatehpur Sikri, 1571−85; the water palace of Shah Quli Khan at Narnaul, 999−1001/1590−93).[11] The

22 *Ajmer, fort of Akbar, 1570, central pavilion. (Photo 1985)*

[9] pp. 52 ff.; the Eng. trans., pp. 37 ff., is not quite reliable with regard to architectural terminology.

[10] See also below, p. 61.

23 *Fatehpur Sikri, Todar Mal's Baradari, between c. 1571 and 1585. (Photo 1985)*

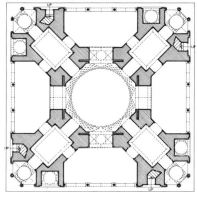

24 *Fatehpur Sikri, Todar Mal's Baradari, ground-plan.*

25 *Narnaul, water palace of Shah Quli Khan, standing in what used to be an artificial lake, 999–1001/1590–93. (Photo 1979)*

[II] For the latter, see Yazdani 1907, pp. 641–43; cf. Parihar, pp. 30–31, pl. 48; for a sketch plan see Soundara Rajan, p. 89.

26 Delhi, Afsarwala mosque and tomb, 1560s. (Photo 1980)

ninefold plan was also employed for mausoleums (tomb of the Hakims at Hasan Abdal in Pakistan, around 1589, on a square plan but with chamfered northwest and southwest corners). The abbreviated version based on an irregular octagon as in the earlier Sabz Burj or Nila Gumbad was preferentially used for tombs, such as the "Afsarwala Gumbad" at Delhi (1560s)[12] or the tomb of Shamshir Khan at Batala in the Panjab (997–98/1588–89), with two-storey niches in all of the outer faces.[13]

Even regular octagonal buildings contain allusions to the ninefold plan in the alternating designs and/or vaulting of the niches in the sides of the tomb or of the ambulatory rooms. A particularly well-thought-out example is the "Hada Mahall" near the Ajmeri Darwaza at Fatehpur Sikri (c. 1570s), where a *hasht bihisht* is inscribed in the regular octagonal plan.[14] A simpler variant is the water palace of Iᶜtimad Khan, now called Burhia ka Tal, at Etmadpur (Iᶜtimadpur) east of Agra (before 1578).[15] Examples of funerary architecture are the tomb of Shah Quli Khan at Narnaul (982/1574–75),[16] the tomb of Hajji Muhammad near the ᶜAmm-Khass Bagh at Sirhind (1014/1605–06), or the Gujaratized version of Nawwab Qutb al-Din Muhammad Khan's tomb at Vadodara (Baroda) (991/1583),[17] now known as the Hajira — a vernacular corruption of *hazira*. The proportions of the latter are broadened to meet the local taste for a rather low and wide building; the outer niches are fitted alternately with typical Gujarati *jali* screens and pierced by passages so as to provide an ambulatory.[18]

The ninefold plan is also found in the *hammam*s of the period (fig. 103).

The exteriors of ninefold-planned buildings, and the variations and abbreviated forms encountered, differ according to their function. As a rule, tombs have an outer dome over the central domed chamber, which in palace

[12] Naqvi, p. 17.

[13] For illus. and further examples see Parihar, p. 32, pl. 29, et passim.

[14] Koch 1987a, pp. 123 ff.

[15] Shah Nawaz Khan, Eng. trans. i, pp. 708 ff.

[16] Yazdani 1907; Parihar, pp. 30 ff., with further examples.

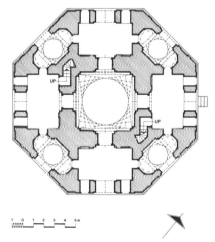

27 Fatehpur Sikri,
Hada Mahall,
between c. 1571 and
1585. (Photo 1985)

28 Fatehpur Sikri,
Hada Mahall,
ground-plan.

[17] The inscription
of the tomb was
identified by Desai
1970b, pp. 70–72.
[18] These features
may account for the
present name of the
tomb. The building
is briefly noted by
Koch 1988a, pp. 170,
176 f.

buildings and gatehouses is masked by a flat roof. In secular architecture one or more *chhatris* may be placed on the roof terrace to act as substitutes for domes.

The inner domes may either be masked by a plaster shell showing the now common decorative arch-netting in the transition zone or be faced with sandstone carved in a corresponding manner. More complex vaults appear in the *hammams* – their decorative stucco shells combine arch-netting with *muqarnas* elements and geometrical patterns (especially combinations of stars and polygons). Of particular interest is the adaptation of a Khurasanian type of vault, which appears in rooms over a cruciform or square ground-plan. It consists of four large intersecting ribs, which create a central vaulted

29 *Etmadpur near Agra, water palace of Ftimad Khan, standing in what used to be an artificial lake, before 1578. At left, on the shore, the tomb of the patron. (Photo 1984)*

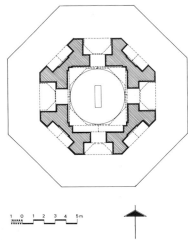

30 *Sirhind, tomb of Hajji Muhammad, 1014/1605–06, ground-plan.*

1 0 1 2 3 4 5m

area, four squinches and four rectangular fields.[19] This multipartite vault form is employed in plaster in the Imperial Hammam of Fatehpur Sikri (1570s). Faced with sandstone it acquires a distinctive local touch in Akbar's *khalwatgah* in the fort of Allahabad (1583),[20] and in the tomb of "the Barber" (999/1590–91) in the garden of Humayun's mausoleum. In the temple of Govind Deva at Vrindavan (1590) constructed by Akbar's noble the Kachhwaha Rajput Man Singh, this vault appears as a brilliant and exciting example of Hindu architecture under Mughal inspiration.[21]

As to the setting, Akbari pleasure-pavilions and tombs were usually placed in gardens which — with the exeption of that of Humayun's tomb — have not survived.

Well preserved, however, are several ensembles belonging to the outstanding group of the water palaces. In Mughal architecture the type only appears in a residential context, though an immediate and impressive forerunner —

[19] For Khurasanian examples see O'Kane, p. 50, et passim.

[20] See below, p. 62.

[21] See below, p. 69.

[22] Koch 1987a, pp. 126 f.

[23] For a plan see Reuther, p. 76; for the date see Desai, 1974, p. 266.

31 Vadodara
(Baroda), tomb of
Qutb al-Din Khan
(Hajira), 991/1583.
(Photo 1978)

Shir Shah Suri's mausoleum at Sasaram in Bihar (1545) – belongs to sepulchral architecture. The Mughals may also have looked for inspiration to the water palaces of the Deccan, where the "Hauz Katora" at Elichpur (late fifteenth or sixteenth century)[22] and the Farah Bagh Palace at Ahmadnagar (1576–83)[23] survive as important examples. The Akbari water palaces adhere to a uniform plan. The main building is situated in the middle of a (usually) artificial rectangular or square reservoir, and can be reached by means of a bridgeway on arches to which access may be provided through a gatehouse on the shore. Two preserved Akbari palaces of this type that were sponsored by nonimperial patrons at Etmadpur and Narnaul have

32 Fatehpur Sikri,
Imperial Hammam,
1570s, vault.
(Photo 1978)

33 Delhi, tomb of the Barber, situated
in the garden of Humayun's tomb,
999/1590–91, interior, vault. (Photo 1981)

34 Delhi,
Humayun's tomb
area, tomb of ʿIsa
Khan Niyazi, an
official of the Sur
rulers, 954/1547–48.
See page 101.
(Photo 1980)

35 Delhi, Mehrauli,
tomb of Adham
Khan, died 1562. See
page 101. (Photo 1979)

already been mentioned (figs. 29, 25). Another example is the water palace of Raja Man Singh at Bairat, probably built in Jahangir's reign.[24]

The Mughals' love of a lifestyle close to nature could lead to even more unusual choices of architectural setting, reminiscent of the Mannerist gardens of the period in Europe. In 982/1574–75 Shah Budagh Khan, when in charge of Mandu in Malwa, constructed the Nilkanth, a plaisance on the mountainside with a magnificent view of the valley below. The architecture consists solely of a U-shaped court with three large *pishtaq*s in the centre of each side. The *pishtaq* of the main axis leads to a grotto-like domed chamber built in the rock over an artificial spring fed from an upper reservoir.[25] The individual forms of the Nilkanth adhere to the Timurid-derived Mughal idiom, with some concessions to the local Malwa style.

The Transoxanian-Timurid influence shows itself most extensively in those building types which were also patronized by the nobility and religious circles, i. e. garden houses and small palaces, secular and religious mausoleums, *hammams*, *karwansara'i*s, and smaller mosques. The main examples of true Akbari synthesis are the great imperial projects, the fortress-palaces and the large *jami^c* mosques.

Fortress-palaces

Almost coeval with the construction of Humayun's tomb was the rebuilding of the old mud-brick fortress of the Lodis at Agra under Qasim Khan (972–980s/1564–1570s; fig. 3/8). The fortification apparently follows the irregular outline of its predecessor. The overall symmetrical planning of imperial residences only became binding in Shah Jahan's reign.[26] In Akbar's period, regular planning of large-scale residential architecture appears to have been

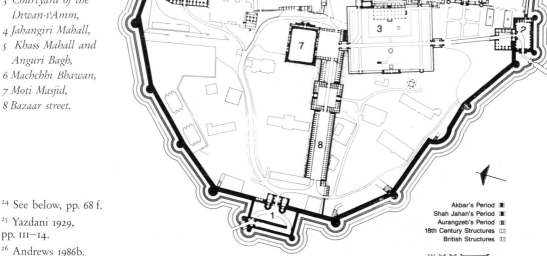

36 Agra fort, plan.
1 Hathi Pol,
2 Amar Singh Gate and Akbari Darwaza,
3 Courtyard of the Diwan-i'Amm,
4 Jahangiri Mahall,
5 Khass Mahall and Anguri Bagh,
6 Machchhi Bhawan,
7 Moti Masjid,
8 Bazaar street.

Akbar's Period
Shah Jahan's Period
Aurangzeb's Period
18th Century Structures
British Structures

[24] See below, pp. 68 f.
[25] Yazdani 1929, pp. 111–14.
[26] Andrews 1986b.

37 Agra fort, Akbari
Darwaza, probably
1566–67, and the
outer Amar Singh
Gate added by
Aurangzib in
1659–62. (Photo 1980)

reserved for the temporary Mughal camp.[27] At Agra, the gates and other
fortificatory elements of earlier Indo-Muslim architecture[28] were brought to
an unsurpassed grandiosity and aesthetic refinement not least by the stun-
ning red sandstone veneer, which gave the structure its present name, Red
Fort. The magnificent Hathi Pol ("Elephant Gate") in the west was the
public entrance. It presents an imposing arcuate facade as showpiece towards
the city and a more informal stepped elevation with trabeate elements
towards the inside of the fort. This scheme was also used subsequently, a particularly impressive example being the famous Buland Darwaza of the great
mosque at Fatehpur Sikri (figs. 60, pl. V).

Only a few structures remain in the Agra fort of the "five hundred
buildings in the wonderful designs of Bengal and Gujarat" of which Akbar's

38 Agra fort, Hathi
Pol, 1568–69.
(Photo 1979)

39 Agra fort,
Jahangiri Mahall, east
(riverside) facade with
central Transoxanian-
style verandah, later
1560s to 1570s.
(Photo 1978)

historian Abu'l Fazl speaks.[29] They seem to have been arranged in a bandlike succession of courtyards along the riverfront, a scheme that was preserved in Shah Jahan's thorough reconstruction. This residential axis was met at
an angle by the (broken) public axis formed by an open bazaar street leading
from the Hathi Pol to the courtyard of public audiences. The most important surviving palace structure of Akbar's period is the main *zanana*
building, misleadingly called "Jahangiri Mahall" ("Jahangir's Palace"; figs.
36/4, pl. IV). A typical example of the wide range of Akbari synthesis, it
features a (later altered) symmetrical ground-plan echoing Timurid plans on
the pattern of Khwaja Ahmad Yasawi's mausoleum at Turkestan (1394–99)[30]
but combines it with the elevation of an open courtyard building. The architectural vocabulary mixes various Transoxanian features, such as the verandah of the east front with its high slender columns   a translation into stone
of the timber *iwan* of vernacular Transoxanian architecture[31] – with courtyard halls styled in the broader Gujarat-Malwa-Rajasthan tradition as it had
been passed on to the Mughals by the early-sixteenth-century architecture of
Raja Man Singh of Gwalior. The Jahangiri Mahall is faced with finely carved
red sandstone. Most of its rooms are not trabeate – as generally assumed –
but present a veritable pattern-book of vaulting of the period: stucco domes
with geometrical patterns and/or arch-netting, ribbed domes and lotus
domes carved in sandstone, pyramidal vaults with a cut top, coved ceilings,
etc. In the handling of the facades we notice the same principle as in the
Hathi Pol. The building presents carefully accentuated arcuate facades
towards the outside, while the inner courtyard fronts are styled in a trabeate
idiom of regional inspiration. That a trabeate unit also appears as centrepiece
of the outer eastern front does not contradict this concept, since the verandah as a literal Transoxanian reference certainly had a special status. The
Mughal architects had by now acquired a firm grip on their diverse architectural repertory and handled it with a distinct sense of its symbolical and
hierarchical potential.

[27] Andrews 1991a.

[28] Burton-Page
1960.

[29] *A'in-i Akbari*,
Eng. trans. ii, p. 191;
cf. Nur Bakhsh
1903–04, pp. 164 ff.;
Ashraf Husain 1937a;
Andrews 1986b.

[30] For illus. see
Golombek and
Wilber, ii, fig. 59.

[31] See above, p. 40,
and Koch 1982b,
pp. 254 f. and
pls. 43a, c.

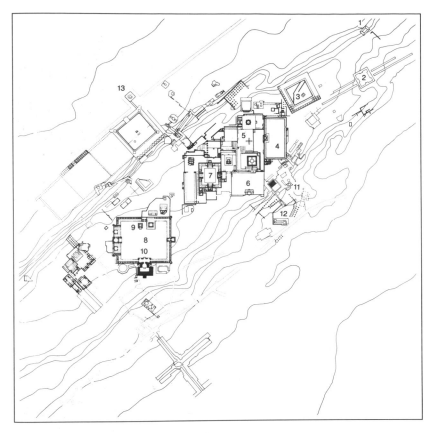

40 Fatehpur Sikri,
c. 1571–85, site-plan.
(Courtesy of
A. Petruccioli)
 1 Tan Sen's Baradari,
 2 Bazaar street with
   char su crossing,
 3 Taksal,
 4 Courtyard
   of Diwan-iᶜAmm,
 5 Semiofficial area
   with Khwabgah,
   Anup Tala'o and
   Diwan-i Khass,
 6 Daftar Khana,
 7 Jodh Ba'i's Palace,
 8 Jamiᶜ Masjid,
 9 Tomb of Shaykh
   Salim Chishti,
10 Buland Darwaza,
11 Imperial
   Hammam,
12 Ba'oli,
13 Hiran Minar.

The rebuilding of the fort of Agra was followed by the construction of the strikingly original Fatehpur Sikri as suburban fortified residence of the court (c. 1571–85).[32] From the stylistic point of view it was Akbar's architectural response to the absorption of Gujarat into the Mughal empire (1572–73). The imperial complex is arranged in an echelon formation on the east-west axis; its irregular layout seems to reflect traditions of Rajput residences. Along this axis three main functional areas can be identified – the courtyard of public audiences or Diwan-i ᶜAmm, the semiofficial area between the "Diwan-i Khass" and the "Khwabgah", and the *zanana* with "Jodh Ba'i's Palace" in its centre. From diverse sources (Gujarat and the Gujarat-Malwa-Rajasthan tradition, the ornamental style of the Delhi Sultanate, Transoxania and Khurasan) the architectural synthesis drew the elements most suitable for a monumental building programme in sandstone, whose affinity with wood favoured the integration of forms derived from timber architecture.

Dominant is the influence of Gujarati Sultanate architecture, which in itself provided a model for a successful synthesis of pre-Islamic Hindu and Jain building traditions.[33] The main organizing principle – trabeate constructions on a grid pattern, extendable to halls or galleries – bears the stamp of Gujarat (cf. Mahmud Begra's palaces at Sarkhej near Ahmadabad, dating from the second half of the fifteenth century). This is also true for the main building type of Fatehpur Sikri, represented most clearly by the white marble tomb of Shaykh Salim Chishti (988/1580–81)[34] in the court of

[32] Of all Mughal architecture, Fatehpur Sikri has attracted the greatest amount of scholarly interest. The standard work is Smith 1894–98; see also Rizvi and Flynn; excellent new plans in Petruccioli 1988. For a recent discussion of the sources of the architecture and the earlier literature see Koch 1987a; for a chronology of the construction see Habib 1987, p. 81; cf. also Andrews 1986b and Burton-Page 1971.

[33] See most recently Koch 1988a.

41 *Diwan-i ʿAmm,*
1570s. (Photo 1980)

42 *Fatehpur Sikri,*
Turkish Sultana's
House, 1570, ceiling
with geometrical
pattern of stars and
hexagons carved in
red sandstone.
(Photo 1985)

43 *Bukhara,*
khanaqa of Khwaja
Zayn al-Din, first
half of 16th century,
ceiling of verandah
with geometrical
pattern of stars and
hexagons carved in
wood. (Photo 1981)

[34] From a careful
reading of Jahangir's
Tuzuk it becomes
plausible that the
whole building, in-
cluding the marble
facing thought to be
of later date, belongs
to Akbar's period;
see Koch 1988a,
p. 170 and n. 2.

[35] Sanderson
1912–13.

the Jamiᶜ Masjid (fig. 40/9). It is modelled closely on the Gujarati tomb par excellence, which consists of an inner (domed) chamber surrounded by a concentric ambulatory verandah of four straight walks, the outside of which is often closed off with latticed marble or sandstone screens (cf. tomb of Shah ᶜAlam at Ahmadabad, 938/1531–32). Even before Fatehpur Sikri, this tomb type had entered Mughal architecture on a grand scale with the mausoleum of Shaykh Muhammad Ghauth at Gwalior (d. 970/1563). A simpler version is the "Nadan Mahall" at Lucknow.[35]

This constructional form also influenced a type of Mughal pavilion with a central block raised above its surrounding verandah (covered by a lean-to roof). The vault of the inner chamber (typical for Fatehpur Sikri is the ribbed

coved ceiling, a convenient vaulting for rectangular halls) was — as usual in
secular structures — concealed on the outside by a flat roof. This design —
which in a residential context had already announced itself in the main
storey of the Bayana pavilion (fig. 12) — was reserved for buildings intended
for the emperor. Thus it was employed for the audience pavilion in the
Diwan-i ᶜAmm (fig. 41) and for the Khwabgah. By inference "Tan Sen's
Baradari" (fig. 40/1) can also be identified as a structure for imperial use, probably a gazebo, since it presented a beautiful view over the (now dried out)
lake of Fatehpur Sikri. A related type is that of the "Daftar Khana" ("Record
Office", most likely the pavilion from whose *jharoka*-window the emperor
showed himself to his subjects), where the closed masonry block and the
verandah of paired pillars embracing it on three sides are of the same height.

46 Gwalior, tomb of
Shaykh Muhammad
Ghauth, died 1563.
(Photo 1978)

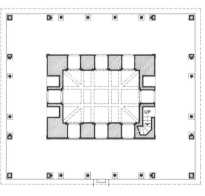

47 Fatehpur Sikri,
Tan Sen's Baradari,
1570s, ground-plan.

48 Fatehpur Sikri,
Tan Sen's Baradari,
pillar of ambulatory
verandah. (Photo 1985)

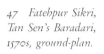

49 Fatehpur Sikri,
Tan Sen's Baradari,
interior with ribbed
coved ceiling.
(Photo 1978)

This juxtaposition of a closed chamber with a pillared porch continued to be influential for Mughal pavilions of later years.

Gujarati influence also makes itself felt in the architectural vocabulary and decor of the palaces of Fatehpur Sikri, in particular in Jodh Ba'i's Palace, the main *zanana* building (fig. 40/7). As a courtyard house on a symmetrical (here four-*iwan*) plan it relates to the Jahangiri Mahall in the Agra fort (fig. 36/4). The much discussed and variously interpreted pillar in the Diwan-i Khass has a giant circular capital composed of two superimposed tiers of serpentine brackets. The design is inspired by Gujarati models, the closest surviving parallels being the surrounding balconies of the minarets of mosques at Ahmadabad (mosque of Sidi Bashir, later fifteenth century).[36]

50 Fatehpur Sikri, Diwan-i Khass, 1570s, central pillar. (Photo 1978)

51 Ahmadabad, mosque of Sidi Bashir, later 15th century, one of the minarets. (Photo 1978)

The utilitarian buildings of Fatehpur Sikri are also influenced by Gujarat. This is true both of water architecture, such as the step-wells (*ba'olis*) and the underground reservoir (*birka*) of the Jami[c] Masjid, and of other public works. The triple-arched gate (*sih taq*) of the crossing (*char su*) of the bazaar of Fatehpur Sikri (begun 984/1576–77; fig. 40/2) is freely based on the Tin Darwaza at Ahmadabad (first half of fifteenth century).

The construction of Agra and Fatehpur Sikri coincides with the foundation of numerous Akbari fortresses all over the rapidly expanding empire, the most important being at Jaunpur (973/1566), Ajmer (978/1570), Lahore (before 1580), Attock or Atak Banaras on the Indus (989/1581), and Allahabad (991/1583). The construction of Fort Nagar Nagar on the Hari Parbat hill at Srinagar, Kashmir, was commenced according to the inscription on its main gate in 1006/1597–98 and brought to completion by Jahangir.

According to Qandahari,[37] the city (*shahr*) of Lahore (which must have included the fort) was completed before 1580. The reconstruction of the Lahore fort by Jahangir and Shah Jahan left little of Akbar's buildings.[38] Certainly from Akbar's reign are the Masti or Masjidi Darwaza (fig. 93/2) and

[36] Koch 1988a, pp. 171, 182–83.

[37] p. 42.

[38] Andrews 1986a.

[39] Reuther, pl. 26; cf. Petruccioli, 1988, 252 E.

52 *Fatehpur Sikri, main bazaar street, begun 1576–77, leading to the Diwan-i'Amm, three-arched gate of the char su crossing. (Photo 1985)*

the (ruined) structures to its northwest, which include a small subterranean octagonal *hammam*. The fortified quadrangle of Akbar's palace at Ajmer (978/1570) is notable for the symmetry of its plan.[39] As also demonstrated by the Jahangiri Mahall of the Agra palace and Jodh Ba'i's Palace at Fatehpur Sikri, such symmetrical layouts were in Akbari palace architecture used in particular for *zanana* courtyard buildings. The wings of the Ajmer fort are formed by single rows of vaulted chambers, which enclose an already mentioned pavilion on an elongated ninefold plan with pillared verandahs (fig. 22). With the latter feature in particular, the pavilion anticipates the Safawid Hasht Bihisht at Isfahan.

53 *Allahabad fort, founded 1583, Rani ki Mahall (Akbar's khalwatgah). (Photo 1980)*

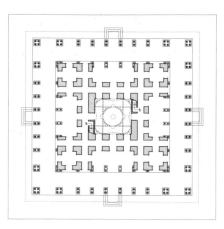

54   Allahabad fort,
Rani ki Mahall,
ground-plan.

The *zanana* enclosure (now walled in by later military structures) in the fort of Allahabad (991/1583) is modelled on the pattern of the Ajmer fort. Its central pavilion, the splendid "Rani ki Mahall" ("Palace of the Queens"), was, according to Abu'l Fazl,[40] Akbar's *khalwatgah-i khass* – his private retiring-room. The Rani ki Mahall enriches the imperial pavilion type of Fatehpur Sikri by the superb pillaring of the surrounding verandah, and by the replacement of the inner rectangular hall by a block on a ninefold plan. The two main pavilion types of the period are thus fused into a convincing whole. The vault over the central hall is the first transformation into sandstone of the Khurasanian vault type rendered in stucco in the Imperial Hammam at Fatehpur Sikri. The "Chalis Sutun" ("Forty-pillared Hall"), a residential tower forming part of the riverside fortifications of the Allahabad fort, is only preserved in a print by the Daniells published in their *Oriental Scenery* (1795–1808). It adapted the stepped trabeate pavilion type to an octagonal plan.[41]

55   Thomas and
William Daniell,
"The Chalees Satoon
in the Fort of
Allahabad on the
River Jumna". From
Oriental Scenery,
1795–1808, series I, 6.
Aquatint.
(Photo British Library
[India Office Library
and Records],
London)

40 *Akbar nama*,
Pers. text iii, p. 415.
41 See also above,
p. 42.

Mosques

The mosques of Akbar's period show the same variety of styles as characterize funerary and residential architecture.[42] The earliest phase continues local traditions while embellishing them with Timurid ideas. The "Khayr al-Manazil" ("Best of Houses") at Delhi, one of the first mosques of the reign, was built by Akbar's wetnurse Maham Anga opposite the Purana Qilᶜa in 969/1561–62.[43] It combines the single-aisle, five-bay Delhi type of Shir Shah's mosque with a courtyard enclosed by three double-storey wings borrowed from Timurid *madrasa*s of the two-*iwan* plan.[44] But for the sandstone-faced *pishtaq* of the eastern gate, the inventiveness of the design of the Khayr al-Manazil is weakened by its execution in the retrospective Lodi idiom.

56 Delhi, Khayr al-Manazil from southeast, 969/1561–62. (Photo 1979)

57 Delhi, Khayr al-Manazil, ground-plan.

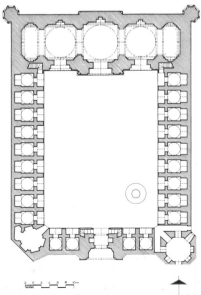

[42] Andrews 1991b.

[43] Zafar Hasan 1915–22, ii, 1919, pp. 51–53.

[44] Cf. *madrasa* of Muhammad Sultan, Samarqand, c. 1400; reconstructed plan in Golombek and Wilber, ii, fig. 27.

58 Delhi, Khayr al-Manazil, mosque, transition zone of central dome. (Photo 1978)

The single-aisle, three-bay mosque of the Delhi Sultanate is adapted by the Mughals and continues to be used as "quarter mosque" (mosque of Shaykh Abd al-Nabi, 983/1575—76, combined with a courtyard)[45] or as funerary mosque in tomb complexes ("Afsarwala" mosque, 1560—67; fig. 26).[46]

One of the first mosques sponsored by Akbar himself is entirely in the Timurid idiom. It is the mosque in the Dargah of Shaykh Muᶜin al-Din Chishti at Ajmer. The evidence suggests that it is one of those buildings commissioned by the emperor on the occasion of his pilgrimage to the shrine in Shaᶜban 977/January 1570.[47] The type of a courtyard mosque with arcaded wings composed of single rows of vaulted bays and a deeper prayer-hall in the west, featuring in the centre the massive block of a large domed

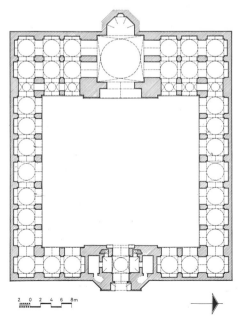

2 0 2 4 6 8m

59 Ajmer, Dargah of Shaykh Muᶜin al-Din Chishti, mosque of Akbar, 1570s, ground-plan.

[45] Zafar Hasan 1921.

[46] Naqvi, p. 16; for examples at Lahore see Chagahtai 1976.

[47] Abu'l Fazl, *Akbar nama,* Eng. trans. ii, pp. 510—11; see also Sarda, p. 87; and Currie, p. 101.

60 *Fatehpur Sikri,*
Jami^c Masjid,
c. 1568–78, courtyard
and inner facade of
Buland Darwaza.
(Photo 1978)

chamber preceded by a high *pishtaq*, had already appeared in the Tughluq architecture of Delhi (Begampuri mosque, c. 1343).[48] In Timurid architecture similar schemes (usually with deeper courtyard wings) were used repeatedly.[49] With the Ajmer mosque, it is as if the prayer-hall of the Humayuni Kachpura mosque at Agra (figs. 4, 5) were enclosed by the courtyard wings of the Begampuri mosque (styled in the Timurid-inspired Kachpura idiom and with only one gate in the eastern wing). The Ajmer prayer-hall is however given a more imposing *pishtaq*, which precedes a high narrow-domed *mihrab* chamber. The court is formed by arcades of dome-covered bays corresponding in height and shape to the bays of the low aisles of the prayer-hall (the inner north and south arcades are a modern addition). The original architectural decoration is obscured by a heavy layer of whitewash.

Akbar's Jami^c Masjid at Fatehpur Sikri (c. 976–85/1568–78) is the first of the "giant open mosques now typical of Mughal cities" (fig. 40/8).[50] Like the imperial residences, this imperial *jami^c* is a showpiece of the great Akbari synthesis. The wings of the great courtyard mosque consist in the north, east and south of *hujra*s (small closet-like rooms) and flat-roofed, pillared galleries. The east and south wings are pierced by monumental gates. On the *qibla* side is a deeper prayer-hall. The immediate source for the design is Indian Sultanate architecture.[51] The plan of a trabeate prayer-hall in which are embedded three domed chambers, the central one preceded by a *pishtaq*, has close relatives in the Atala mosque at Jaunpur (1376–1408) and the mosques of Gujarat. The latter also provided the models for the supports of the prayer-hall and their irregular spacing and for the articulation of the arched screens facing the galleries of the courtyard wings. The somewhat

[48] For a plan and illus. see Welch and Crane, p. 130, fig. 1, pls. 3, 4.

[49] Golombek and Wilber, cat. nos. 5, 28, 48, 78, 90, 123.

[50] Andrews 1981, p. 110.

[51] For comparative plans see Petruccioli 1988, figs. 258 A, D, E

retrospective character of the scheme is relieved by the red sandstone and by the *pishtaq*s in the recent Delhi fashion, which reach new, staggering proportions in the Buland Darwaza ("Lofty Gate"; pl. V). Its total height above ground of c. 54 m surpasses even the famous *iwan*s of Akbar's megalomaniac ancestor Timur in Shahr-i Sabz and Samarqand.

A masterpiece of Mughal engineering is Mun^cim Khan's bridge at Jaunpur (976/1569).[52] From the early 1570s particular emphasis was given to public works along the highways, such as wells, reservoirs and *karwansara'i*s, a programme based on the "spadework" of Shir Shah Suri. The imperial

Public and
utilitarian buildings

61 Jaunpur, bridge of Mun^cim Khan, 976/1569. (Photo 1981)

62 Kos minar near Ajmer on the Ajmer-Jaipur road. (Photo 1985)

[52] Führer 1889, pp. 17–21.
[53] W. Finch in Foster, pp. 148 ff.
[54] Rabbani.
[55] Husain, pp. 117–29.

pilgrimage road from Agra to Ajmer was lined at regular intervals with stations for imperial use,[53] and small *minars* functioning not only as milestones but also as hunting memorials of the emperor, since they were originally studded with the horns of animals he shot. They represent a smaller form of the Akbari hunting-towers that were set up in imitation of Iranian models based on an ancient tradition,[54] e. g. the "Hiran Minar" at Fatehpur Sikri (fig. 40/13), the "Chor Minar" at Delhi or the "Nim Sara'i Minar" at Malda in eastern Bengal (today Bangladesh).[55]

The typical plan of the Mughal *karwansara'i* (usually termed *sara'i*) that emerges at this time (Sara'i Chhata north of Mathura, Sara'i Chhaparghat

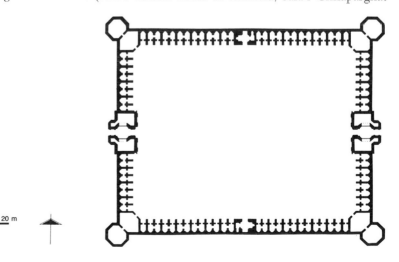

0   20 m

south of Kannauj and southwest of Kanpur) did not vary much in later periods.[56] The plan is uniform in principle. It consists of a square or rectangular compound formed by wings of unconnected tiny closet-like rooms (*hujra*) with a narrow porch (the Mughal *iwan*), a scheme that was also used in the wings of mosques functioning as *madrasas* (Khayr al-Manazil at Delhi, Jamic Masjid of Fatehpur Sikri). In the centre of those wings that have no gates is a block of larger rooms for the use of higher-ranking persons. The corners are fortified with towers, which may contain larger apartments, *hammams*, or storerooms. If the *sara'i* has not one but two gates, these face each other and are often connected by a bazaar street. The outer fronts of the gates are – as showpieces of the *sara'i* – given special architectural attention. A small mosque and one or two wells complete the building programme.

As to stables, there is very little surviving evidence. The courtyard enclosure traditionally known as the "Taksal" ("Mint") at Fatehpur Sikri (fig. 40/3) appears to have been a stable according to the evidence provided by recent excavations.[57] The building has four wings with a single doorway in the southeast side. The wings consist of two rectangular concentric rows of domed bays demarcated by arches on cruciform piers (half-piers on the outer wall). The inner piers are pierced by a narrow ambulatory corridor, a feature that speaks for the stable interpretation, since it would allow grooms easy access to each bay (or box). Such four-wing complexes were thus a staple design of Mughal architecture, which could be used – with minor adjustments – for quite diverse purposes.

The bazaars consist of open streets lined by wings made of the same elements as the *karwansara'i*s, namely *hujra*s and porches; they may have a crossing with four gates called *char su* (Agra fort, fig. 36/8; Fatehpur Sikri, fig. 40/2). Father Monserrate, the chronicler of the first Jesuit mission to the court of Akbar (1580–83), mentions a bazaar in the citadel of Lahore with a high pitched timber roof.[58]

The *hammams* of the period are best represented by those of Fatehpur Sikri; they constitute what is probably the largest surviving concentration of *hammams* dating from a single period and in a single place in all of Islamic architecture.[59] We know from Shah Jahan's authors that a Mughal *hammam* was to have three functional units, a *rakht kan* (dressing-room), a *sard khana* (cold room) and a *garam khana* (hot room). Not mentioned are the latrines that were provided in all *hammams*. There was no architectural norm for the shape and arrangement of these individual units. They could be anything from a single chamber to a group of interconnecting rooms.

The Kachhwaha Rajput Man Singh was an enthusiastic patron of architecture; his buildings combine Rajput traditions with the Mughal style. During his governorship of Bengal (1594–1607) he, a Hindu, even sponsored a large mosque at Rajmahall (Akbarnagar). Man Singh's palaces at Rohtasgarh in Bihar (late sixteenth century)[60] and Amber near Jaipur reflect imperial Mughal palaces. The *zanana* courtyard of the Rohtas palace follows the scheme employed at Ajmer and Allahabad of narrow residential wings sur-

Subimperial patronage

66 Bairat, water palace standing in what used to be an artificial lake, attributed to Raja Man Singh Kachhwaha, early 17th century. (Photo 1982)

rounding a large pavilion. The water palace at Bairat northeast of Jaipur (early seventeenth century),[61] which on account of its stylistic parallels to Man Singh's palace at Amber can be safely attributed to the same patron, copies that of Shah Quli Khan at Narnaul (fig. 25). Of particular interest is a group of temples at Vrindavan near Mathura, connected to Kachhwaha patronage (pl. VI) because they succeed in adapting the style of Fatehpur Sikri to the

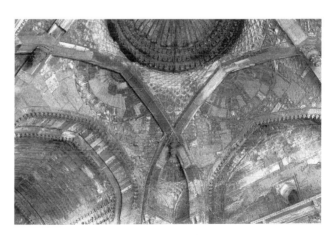

67 Vrindavan, temple of Govind Deva, vault over crossing, 1590. (Photo 1978)

requirements of Hindu religious architecture.[62] Outstanding here is the vault over the crossing of Man Singh's temple of Govind Deva (begun in 1590), a giant sandstone version of the Khurasanian vault type based on four intersecting arches.[63] That the most daring vault construction of north Indian architecture of the sixteenth century should appear in a temple sheds a significant light on the architectural open-mindedness of the period.

In the following periods, too, the Kachhwaha Rajputs continued to be the closest followers of the Mughal imperial style in their building enterprises in Amber and Jaipur.[64]

[56] The pioneering study of I. A. Khan is forthcoming in the *Indian Historical Review.*

[57] "Explorations and Excavations: Uttar Pradesh", in *Indian Archaeology 1981–82: A Review,* pp. 63 f., fig. 8.

[58] Latin text, p. 622; Eng. trans. p. 160.

[59] For plans see Petruccioli 1988, figs. 131, 137.

[60] Description and plans in Kuraishi, pp. 146–83.

[61] Koch 1983, p. 186, n. 76, fig. 23.

[62] Growse, pp. 241–57.

[63] See above, p. 50; and Koch 1987a, pp. 137 ff.

[64] Tillotson, pp. 93 ff., 167 ff.

After the phase of architectural syncretism under Akbar, there follows with Jahangir's reign a period of transition, reflection and experimentation which – despite its importance for the future development of Mughal architecture – has not yet received due acknowledgement. Selected ideas of the previous periods are now adopted in formal extravaganzas that had a negligible echo or developed into highly influential models.

Typical of the period are highly decorated surfaces of buildings (exterior and interior). The walls are often deeply panelled by a framework of bands. Architectural decoration is characterized by a plethora of materials: the familiar sandstone carving (which attains a new refinement), white marble, stone intarsia, painted stucco, and tile-work. The favourite motif of wall decoration, regardless of the technique, is the *chini khana* ("china room"). It consists of small blind or real niches, usually of a multi-lobed constricted shape, which contain bottles and/or flower-vases. This motif may also appear in dense configurations covering the whole surface of a wall (fig. 100). Figurative representations are also popular, in particular wall-paintings "drawne from Europe prints (of which they make accompt heere)" (pl. VIII).[1]

New solutions are tried out in the vaults. Characteristic are intricately patterned stucco vaults that fuse (or replace) the earlier arch-netting with a new pseudostructural network system developed from points (often stars) arranged in concentric circles.[2] These patterns appear to have been inspired by Safawid sources (based in turn on Timurid forerunners),[3] which became influential in this period. Typical of Jahangiri vaults is that the network generates fan-like formations of lozenge-shaped *muqarnas* (fig. 83). Another specific technique of lining domes – almost exclusive to Jahangir's period – is that of oversailing concentric tiers of small arched *muqarnas* (fig. 85).

Several of the above features already appear in Jahangir's first building enterprise after his accession, the now traditional construction of his father's mausoleum at Sikandra, a suburb of Agra (1022/1613, pl. IX). The place was renamed Bihishtabad ("Paradise Town") to honour its new status as burial-place of the great emperor.[4] The tomb of Akbar stands in the centre of a classical *char bagh*, whose main *khiyaban*s terminate in one real and three blind gates. The latter are derived from the Akbari type with an arcuate outer and a stepped inner front. The intention of the prototype is here however inverted, as the *pishtaq*ed fronts face inwards. This must not necessarily be seen as mannerist wilfulness, but rather as a successful scenographic device: as it were, the voids of the *pishtaq*s absorb the *khiyaban*s of the garden.

The overall concept of the mausoleum, which is placed at the crossing of the two principal *khiyaban*s, is at the same time retrospective and unorthodox – a congenial response of sepulchral architecture to the great architectural synthesis of the mosque and palace projects of the late emperor.

Tombs

[1] Mundy, p. 215.

[2] Koch 1983 and 1986a.

[3] Similar vaults can be found in the small palace at Nayin (sixteenth century), see Luschey-Schmeisser.

[4] Kanbo, i, p. 14; for a description and plans see Smith 1909.

68 *Agra, Sikandra, tomb of Akbar, 1022/1613, southern gate seen from south. (Photo 1978)*

69 *Agra, Sikandra, tomb of Akbar, site-plan. (After E. W. Smith)*

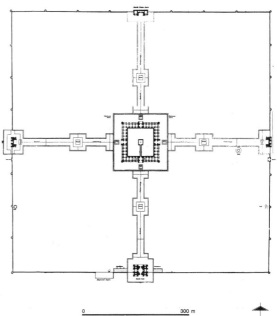

0   300 m

The tomb combines the Timurid-inspired vaulted masonry trend —
represented by the podium (containing domed bays and a vestibule with
painted plaster decoration [pl. VII]) and its high *pishtaq*s (decorated with
stone intarsia producting the effect of tile-work) — with the indigenous
trabeate sandstone mode represented by the receding storeys of pillared
galleries. The scheme once again demonstrates the close relationship between
residential and sepulchral architecture in that it brings the stepped pavilion
type of the previous periods on to the grand scale of imperial tombs — and,
at the same time, to a dead end. Future trends announce themselves in the
hierarchical use of white marble for the topmost open storey of the
mausoleum and in the minarets topping the southern gatehouse.[5] We here
encounter the first use of multiple minarets in Mughal architecture, to
become a distinctive feature in the period of Shah Jahan. Another noteworthy aspect of the southern gate is its particularly rich stone intarsia-work
echoing — together with that of the blind gates — the decoration of the
*pishtaq*s of the tomb.

Stone intarsia had already established itself unter Akbar as an important
branch of Mughal architectural decoration. The tomb of Atga Khan
(974/1566–67) at Nizamuddin, Delhi, had been a particularly remarkable instance of Timurid tile mosaic patterns being transposed into stone intarsia.[6]
Further impressive early examples are the Akbari Darwaza and Hahti Pol

70 Delhi,
Nizamuddin, tomb of
Atga Khan,
974/1566–67.
(Photo 1978)

of the Agra fort (later 1560s; figs. 37, 38). The craft was further developed and
refined under Jahangir and Shah Jahan.[7]

The design of Akbar's mausoleum had no direct influence, through the
contemporary tomb of Shah Begam (d. 1605), the mother of Jahangir's ill-
fated son Khusrau, in the Khusrau Bagh at Allahabad[8] bears a clear family
relationship: its two solid receding storeys are crowned by an open-pillared
chhatri (fig. 81).

The principle of setting a group of lighter superstructures on a massive
podium (*takhtgah*) with vaulted bays or rooms continues to be a definite
trend in the sepulchral architecture of Jahangir's period. The concept had
already announced itself towards the end of Akbar's reign in the tomb of
Sadiq Muhammad Khan Herati at Dholpur (1005–06/1596–97), built in a
garden near his house and *sara'i*, now in ruins.[9] The design appears here in

[5] Burton-Page 1991b; Husain, pp. 185 f.

[6] Zafar Hasan 1922, pp. 31 f.

[7] See below, pp. 75, 95.

[8] For dates see Desai 1961, pp. 64–68.

[9] Shah Nawaz Khan, Eng. trans. ii, p. 662. Today the tomb is almost unknown, despite having been publish-ed with a plan, drawings and a reading of its inscrip-tion as early as in the *Transactions of the Archaeological Society of Agra* (January to June 1875, Appendix, pp. i–iv).

its most basic form, namely that of a funerary platform, of regular octagonal shape. The superstructures are limited to a second smaller octagonal platform in the centre, surrounded by a (fragmentarily surviving) latticed screen with a small gate-kiosk, and pillared kiosks on the periphery. The sepulchral form of an open platform surrounded by a screen[10] was perhaps chosen out of an orthodox conviction on the part of the patron to circumvent the Prophet's apocryphal condemnation of funerary structures. This consideration might indeed have led to the creation of the Mughal *takhtgah* tomb. The original intention was, however, at times again contradicted by a domed structure placed on the platform.

Further remarkable features of the tomb of Sadiq Khan are the fine craftsmanship of the remains of the screen and the paving of the surface of the central podium with white marble and black and variegated yellow stone in

72 Agra, tomb attributed to Firuz Khan, first third of 17th century. (Photo 1978)

[10] Golombek (1969, pp. 100–124) discusses this tomb type in the Timurid context and describes it as a *hazira*.

a geometrical pattern; the stone and colour combinations herald a typical trend of future Mughal stone intarsia.

The octagonal form of the platform tomb was taken up again and further evolved in the tomb of Firuz Khan on the Gwalior Road at Agra. The structure set in the centre of the platform is here a domed octagon. The peripheral structures are placed in the cardinal directions. They consists in the west of a miniature mosque and in the east of a gate construction raised from the ground floor level; it has a steep stairway leading up to the platform (Mughal architects usually treated stairs as a necessary evil). The gate has an elaborate facing of carved sandstone showing characteristic Jahangiri motifs, ornamental cartouches along with blind niches containing not only vessels but also birds in relief-work.[11]

73 Agra, tomb of Firuz Khan, gate. (Photo 1978)

The square version of the platform tomb is represented by the "tomb of Maryam al-Zamani" (d. 1032/1623), Jahangir's mother, at Sikandra, Agra.[12] It has superstructures in the form of octagonal *chhatris* above the corners and oblong ones above the centres of the sides.

The scheme finds its most elegant expression in the tomb of I^{c}timad al-Daula, Jahangir's *wazir* and the father of his favourite and powerful wife, Nur Jahan, at Agra (1036–37/1626–28; fig. 3/4). The superstructures here take the form of round turret-like kiosks at the corners and a square pavilion with a canopied dome in the centre. The peculiar shape of the domed roof is derived from wooden canopies over the tombs of Sufi shaykhs, which had already been transposed into white marble in the catafalque of the mausoleum of Shaykh Muhammad Ghauth at Gwalior. The rooms of the ground-floor podium of It^{c}imad al-Daula's tomb are arranged according to a ninefold plan.

[11] Nath (1976a, pp. 120–128) dates the tomb in the early reign of Shah Jahan, while conceding that it is stylistically indebted to Jahangiri architecture.

[12] For description, plans and illus. see Sanderson 1910–11, pp. 94–96, pls. 48–50; in the older literature the building is erroneously identified with a *baradari* of Sikander Lodi.

74 Agra, Sikandra, tomb attributed to Maryam al-Zamani, died 1623. (Photo 1978)

Several features of the tomb anticipate characteristic trends of the architecture of Shah Jahan: the vaults of the central chamber and of the corner rooms in a network pattern developed from points arranged in concentric circles; the coved ceilings of the verandahs and of the upper pavilion; the cladding of the entire outside of the building with white marble inlaid with different-coloured stones. The latter technique (which has Indo-Islamic forerunners in Gujarat)[13] represents a further step from the earlier simple stone intarsia (used so conspicuously on the *pishtaq*s and gates of Akbar's mausoleum) towards the more refined Italianate *commesso di pietre dure* technique of Shah Jahan's buildings.[14]

Of the tomb types inherited from the previous period, the Gujarat-derived tomb type with a central domed block and a (lower) ambulatory verandah

75 Agra, tomb of I'timad al-Daula, 1036–37/1626–28. (Photo 1979)

[13] Koch 1987b, pp. 39–44.

[14] Smith 1901, pp. 18–20. See also below, p. 95.

remains in fashion (tomb of Baha' al-Din near the Tehra Darwaza at Fatehpur Sikri, 1019/1610–11). The verandahs are often accentuated with allusions to the prevailing ninefold plan by a division of the ceilings and/or the spacing of the supports. In the tomb of Shaykh Pir at Meerut (probably 1022/1613)[15] the central block is given on the outside the appearance of a two-storey building by two superimposed rows of arched *jali*ed openings. The verandah that surrounded the "ground floor" is almost completely destroyed. The building is remarkable for the high craftsmanship employed in the ornamentation of its red sandstone facing with carved motifs, *jali* screens and intarsia with white marble. Some of the motifs are used with great licence, such as the flower-vases in relief that appear instead of arch-netting on the pendentives of the dome. Unorthodox as this motif may seem, it was taken up by Shahjahani architects, for instance in the mosque of Fatehpuri Begam near the Taj Mahall at Agra, or in the imperial baldachin of marble projecting from the south wing of the Machchhi Bhawan in the Agra palace (completed 1637; fig. 123).

Also within this group is the tomb of Makhdum Shah Daulat at Maner (1025/1616) west of Patna in Bihar.[16] It is conceived along the lines of the tomb of Muhammad Gauth at Gwalior, but true to the fashion of the period it is placed — together with a gate and a mosque — on a podium with corner towers. The tomb of Iraj Shah Nawaz (d. 1028/1618–19), son of the great commander ʿAbd al-Rahim Khan-i Khanan, at Burhanpur and the tomb of Iftikhar Khan (d. 1021/1612–13) at Chunar near Varanasi (Benares) represent the massive arcuate version of this tomb type. The surrounding gallery of the latter shows unique tunnel-vaults of a horseshoe-arch profile; since this

76 Gwalior, tomb of Muhammad Gauth, died 1563, interior catafalque. (Photo 1978)

77 Meerut, tomb of Shaykh Pir, probably 1613, interior. (Photo 1978)

[15] Jahangir, Eng. trans. i, pp. 241, 346.
[16] Kuraishi, pp. 61–66.

78 Burhanpur, tomb of Shah Nawaz Khan, died 1618–19. (Photo 1984)

79 Chunar, tomb attributed to Iftikhar Khan Turkman, died 1612–13. (Photo 1979)

80 Delhi, tomb of ᶜAbd al-Rahim Khan-i Khanan, died 1627. (Photo 1978)

unusual feature bears a close resemblance to *chaitya* arches it may represent an appreciation of the ancient Buddhist remains in the area.

The cube-shaped Delhi type of tomb (which in Akbar's period was represented for instance by the tomb of Atga Khan, 974/1566—67, at Nizamuddin, Delhi)[17] continues to be used. Important examples are the mausoleum of ʿAbd al-Rahim Khan-i Khanan at Delhi (d. 1036/1627),[18] which incorporates a not fully developed ninefold plan, and those in the Khusrau Bagh at Allahabad: the tomb of Sultan Nithar Begam, sister of Khusrau (1034/1624—25), and the tomb of Khusrau (d. 1031/1622).[19] The latter has not the usual *pishtaq* in the centre of each side but — like the central

81 *Allahabad, Khusrau Bagh, tomb of Shah Begam (died 1605). (Photo 1978)*

82 *Allahabad, Khusran Bagh, tombs of Sultan Nithar Begam (1034/1624—25) and of Sultan Khusrau (died 1622). (Photo 1978)*

[17] See above, p. 72.

[18] Zafar Hasan 1915—22, ii, 1919, pp. 128 f.

[19] See above, p. 72.

block of Shaykh Pir's tomb – superimposed niches all around that create the impression of two storeys. All Allahabad tombs have excellent stucco vaults patterned with network, developed from stars arranged in concentric circles with clusters of lozenge-shaped *muqarnas*.

The octagonal tombs present a heterogeneous picture. Among the already discussed octagonal versions of the *takhtgah* or platform tomb may, in the widest sense, also be counted the tomb of "Tambulan Begam", in the Khusrau Bagh at Allahabad. The ground floor has the shape of an octagonal podium housing a cruciform chamber; the superstructure consists of a single octagonal domed kiosk. The concept almost literally repeats that of the

83   Allahabad, Khusrau Bagh, tomb of Sultan Nithar Begam, interior, dome. (Photo 1980)

84   Allahabad, Khusrau Bagh, tomb of Tambulan Begam, first quarter of 17th century. (Photo 1978)

85 *Allahabad, Khusrau Bagh, tomb of Tambulan Begam, interior of sepulchral pavilion. (Photo 1980)*

earlier water pavilion at Etmadpur (fig. 29); the analogies between tombs and garden pavilions are here very apparent.[20] The inner dome of the tomb of Tambulan Begam rests like a baldachin on eight arches rising from floor level. The dome is of interest because above the arch-netted zone it is lined with oversailing tiers of arched (flattened) *muqarnas*, a form peculiar to Jahangiri architecture.

The tomb of Muhammad Wasit in the Dargah of Shah Qasim Sulaymani at Chunar (1028/1618) represents a more monumental version of the tomb of Tambulan Begam with its proportions changed in favour of the superstructure and with four *pishtaq*s alternating with four lower blind arches; a *chhajja* emphasizes the changing levels of the façade elements.[21]

The tomb of "the Ustad" (actually that of Muhammad Mu'min Husayn) at Nakodar in the Panjab (1021/1612−13) belongs to the group that continues the irregular octagonal tomb type of Akbar's period.[22]

The most outstanding and ingeniously planned octagonal building, not only of Jahangir's period but − next to Humayun's tomb − in the whole history of Mughal architecture, is the mausoleum of "Anarkali" at Lahore (completed 1024/1615). So far the building has mainly attracted attention for being the sepulchre of a beloved of Jahangir. This scholarly neglect may be due to the fact that the tomb − which originally stood in large, architecturally planned gardens − was considerably modified in being adapted for use as a Christian church in 1851; it is now the Panjab Records Office.[23] The building has the outer shape of an irregular octagon, with octagonal towers at its points that project as half-octagons topped by octagonal *chhatri*s. Inscribed in the figure is a radial ninefold plan with two patterns of cross axes (+ and x). A similar configuration of rooms inscribed in an octagon had

[20] Such parallels appear to have misled Burton-Page (1991a, pp. 127−28) into describing both the water pavilion of I'timad Khan and that of Shah Quli Khan at Narnaul as "fine but anonymous examples" of funerary architecture. The actual tombs of both patrons are separate structures erected in both cases near the shore of the artifical lakes. See our fig. 29.

[21] Illus. in Daniell, Series III, no. 23, as "Mausoleum of Kausim Solemanee."; cf. Führer 1891, p. 259.

[22] Parihar, p. 34 f., pl. xi.

[23] The building has been published with a plan and an elevation but with only a very brief description by A. N. Khan 1980b.

already appeared in the Hada Mahall at Fatepur Sikri (fig. 28), but here the
rooms on the x-axis were not connected with the main domed hall. That the
tomb of Anarkali is a truly outstanding design can be seen by comparing
it with related solutions of Western architecture. It is as if Michelangelo's last
design for San Giovanni de' Fiorentini in Rome (1559) had been fitted into
the outline of Frederick II's Castel del Monte in Apulia (c. 1240)!

87 Lahore, tomb
of Anarkali,
completed
1024/1615,
reconstructed
ground-plan.

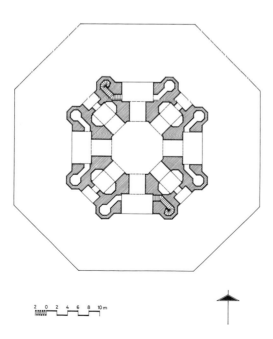

2 0 2 4 6 8 10 m

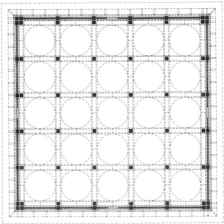

*88 Delhi, Nizamuddin, Chaunsath Khamba (tomb of Mirza
ᶜAziz Koka, died 1623–4). (Photo 1978)*

A new type of mausoleum in Jahangir's period is that of the flat-roofed
arched hypostyle hall composed of domed bays demarcated by pillars or
piers arranged in a grid pattern. The scheme had announced itself already
in the single-aisle pillared hall of the "Solah Khamba" at Lucknow;[24] now
it appears fully developed, with pillars set in pairs around the periphery, in
the white marble mausoleum of Mirza ᶜAziz Koka (d. 1033/1623–24), the
"Chaunsath Khamba", at Nizamuddin, Delhi.[25] The white marble *jali*s that
close it off to the outside point to Gujarat as the most likely source of inspiration for such halls. The design was repeated in red sandstone without
*jali*s in the tomb of "Salabat Khan" between Sikandra and Agra.

*89 Delhi,
Nizamuddin,
Chaunsath Khamba,
ground-plan.*

*90 Agra, tomb
attributed to Salabat
Khan, second quarter
of 17th century.
(Photo 1978)*

Similar tendencies also appear in the mosque architecture of the period. The "Patthar Masjid" ("Stone Mosque") at Srinagar (1620s?), sponsored according to tradition by Jahangir's wife Nur Jahan, has three aisles parallel to the *qibla* wall, each consisting of nine bays demarcated by massive cruciform piers and coved ceilings or vaults with the intricate patterns characteristic of the period. Such arched halls on a grid pattern foreshadow a definite trend of the mosque and palace architecture of Shah Jahan.

91 Srinagar, Patthar Masjid, c. 1620s, ground-plan.

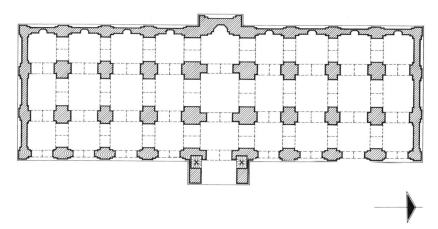

The compact masonry mosque of the Delhi tradition embellished with Timurid and Safawid components is best represented by another mosque of female patronage, that of Jahangir's mother Maryam al-Zamani at Lahore (1020–23/1611–14).[26] The prayer-hall of the Begam Shahi Mosque, as it is commonly called, is a single-aisle five-bay structure with an elaborate painted decoration. Its inner central dome reveals one of the first dated occurrences of a network developed from points arranged in concentric circles.

The courtly mosque architecture of Jahangir's period thus bears the stamp of female patronage; the emperor himself did not sponsor any major mosque projects.

92 Lahore, Begam Shahi Masjid, 1020–23/1611–14, ground-plan.

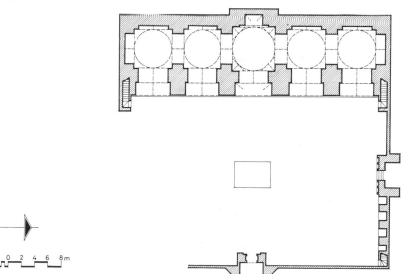

[24] Plans and illus. in Sanderson 1912–13.

[25] Zafar Hasan 1922, pp. 34 f.

[26] A. N. Khan 1972.

Jahangir's preferred projects were in the domain of palace and garden architecture. Most were however either altered or demolished by his son and successor Shah Jahan, who considered them "old-fashioned and of bad design" (*kuhnagī wa bad ṭarḥī*).[27] To the latter belong Jahangir's additions to the palace of Agra.

The best picture of urban Jahangiri palace architecture can be obtained in the fort of Lahore,[28] which Jahangir began to reconstruct after his accession. The final touch was given to the buildings between 1617 and 1620 by Jahangir's architect ᶜAbd al-Karim Maᶜmur Khan. He had recommended himself for this task by his successful adaptation of the palaces of the Malwa sultans at Mandu for the stay of the court in 1617.[29] Although the palace of Lahore did not escape later alterations, the greater part of the constructions between Akbar's Diwan-i ᶜAmm courtyard and the riverfront date from Jahangir's reign. They consist of narrow wings (laid around open courtyards) constructed according to the local fashion in brick, and plastered and painted with various designs in the typical colours of the period: white, light green, dark red and ochre.

"Jahangir's Quadrangle", the main *zanana* courtyard, combines the local brick architecture with quotations from the imperial style of Agra and Fatehpur Sikri in the form of trabeate sandstone verandahs. The *chhajja* of the courtyard wings is supported by composite zoomorphic brackets in the shape of elephants, felines and peacocks. Such unorthodox features were now

Palaces

93 Lahore fort, plan. (After the recent plan of the Superintendent of Archaeology, Western Pakistan Circle, Lahore, but with the Shah Burj complex remeasured and with some different attributions of building phases) 1 ᶜAlamgiri Darwaza, 2 Masti Darwaza, 3 Shah Burj, 4 Kala Burj, 5 Shah Jahan's marble building, 6 Jahangir's Quadrangle, 7 Moti Masjid, 8 Courtyard of Diwan-i ᶜAmm.

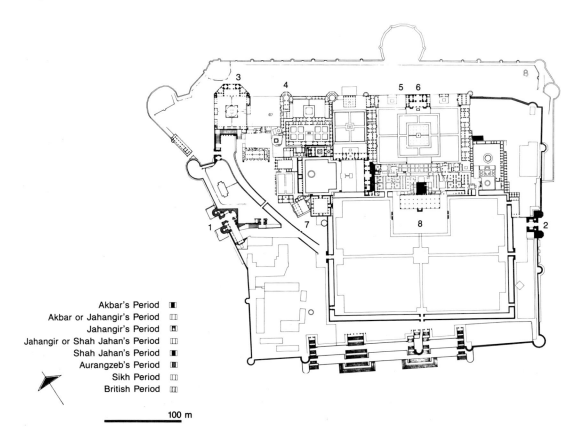

Akbar's Period
Akbar or Jahangir's Period
Jahangir's Period
Jahangir or Shah Jahan's Period
Shah Jahan's Period
Aurangzeb's Period
Sikh Period
British Period

100 m

94 *Lahore fort, Jahangir's Quadrangle, completed 1620, west wing. (Photo 1979)*

considered tolerable not only in the informal atmosphere of the *zanana*, but also in less private areas, where they appear in the form of figurative wall-paintings. The vault of the "Kala Burj", a residential tower, preserves wall-paintings characteristic of the extravagant Jahangiri taste: a Solomonic programme of birds and angels, including putti after European models (pl. VIII).[30] Related subjects appear in an unusually exposed position on the outer walls of the riverside and west fronts of the fort: the multi-panelled surface contains court scenes, animal-fights and mythical figures in tile mosaic.[31]

At Delhi, Jahangir ordered the construction of palace buildings in the small fort of Salimgarh,[32] which was now renamed Nurgarh. These buildings (completed in 1619, no longer extant) accommodated the court when it passed through Delhi until Shah Jahan's completion of the new fortress-palace of Shahjahanabad (opposite the Salimgarh) in 1648 (figs. 127, 129).

Besides these additions to the palaces in the Mughal metropolises, Jahangir also built several country houses and hunting-lodges. The most outstanding is Shaikhupura near Lahore (1015–30/1607–20; pl. XI), a classical octagonal water pavilion of the design of the Sher Mandal (fig. 11) in a large artificial tank, the corners of which are accentuated by small kiosks. The main pavilion is linked by a bridgeway on arches to a gatehouse on the western bank.[33] The highly picturesque ensemble thus repeats all the elements of the earlier Akbari water palaces, albeit on a grander scale. A new feature is the hunting-tower that stands not far away, on the axis of the bridgeway. To judge from holes in its surface, it was originally decorated with trophies in the tradition of Akbar's hunting-memorials.[34] It is significant that the earliest surviving hunting-palaces of the Mughals date from Jahangir's time (Akbar's Nagarchin is not preserved, or has not yet been identified). From the abundant references in his memoirs, the *Tuzuk*, Jahangir appears to have been the most enthusiastic hunter among the first six Mughal emperors, who all – including Aurangzib – attached great importance to the sport.

Another of Jahangir's country houses in a highly picturesque setting was the Chashma-i Nur in the hills west of Ajmer, completed in 1024/1615

[27] Lahori, i/2, p. 51, et passim

[28] Andrews 1986a.

[29] Jahangir, i, pp. 363 f., 368, 375 f.

[30] Koch 1983.

[31] Vogel

[32] Jahangir, ii, 109.

[33] A. N. Khan 1980a.

[34] Rabbani

(pl. X).[35] Here particular attention was given to relating the architecture to the hilly site and to the spectacular water-lift, an (unfinished) stepped structure said to have been built by Rao Maldeva of Marwar in 1535 to conduct water upwards. The chief relic of Jahangir's complex is a high masonry *pishtaq* – standing in a defile between two hillsides – with a basin at its foot. The *pishtaq* provides access to a grotto in the mountainside, the concept being reminiscent of the Nilkanth at Mandu. In 1616 Sir Thomas Roe, the English ambassador to the court of Jahangir, described the Chashma (also known as Hafiz Jamal) as "a place of much melancholy delight",[36] thus anticipating the sentiments of many a later English traveller to India in search of the picturesque.

The emperor's main interest was here directed to the development of Kashmir as summer residence of the court. One of Jahangir's first projects after his accession was the laying out of a garden around the source of the Jehlam (Behat) at Vernag. His visit in 1620 sparked off a whole wave of garden projects, among them the Nur Afza in the fort of Hari Parbat, Achabal (altered by Shah Jahan's daughter Jahanara between 1634 and 1640), and the lower garden, the Farah Bakhsh ("Joy-Imparting") of the famous Shalimar. The construction of the latter was put in the hands of Prince Khurram, the latter Shah Jahan,[37] who had by this time proven his talent for architecture.

Gardens

The central feature of the Mughal garden at Kashmir is a spring, whose waters are collected in a canal (*nahr*) that forms the main axis of the garden. The layout takes advantage of the sloping hillside site for terraces (*martaba*), ponds (*hauz*), branch canals (*jadwal, juy*) and pavilions and platforms (*nashiman*) sited along the watercourse.[38]

Other members of the imperial family and grandees of the court also laid out numerous gardens. After the death of their owners these reverted to the crown; the emperor either kept them for himself or bestowed them on members of his family and the nobility. The same garden would thus pass through a chain of successive owners, which led to repeated remodelling and renaming.

The same applies to the gardens of Agra, at least those which were not converted by their owners into tomb gardens to prevent them falling into the emperor's hands. Agra's development as a city of riverside gardens seems to have been given special attention in this period. Of the thirty-three gardens listed with their names by Pelsaert in 1626,[39] about one-third were created or refashioned during Jahangir's reign. This is particularly true of the river bank north of Iʿtimad al-Daula's tomb, which boasts one of the best-preserved residential gardens not only of Agra but, next to the Farah Bakhsh, of Jahangir's period altogether. It is the "Ram Bagh", by a twentieth century tradition associated with Babur, but now re-identified as Nur Jahan's Bagh-i Nur Afshan, completed in 1621 (fig. 3/1).[40]

By this time the (residential) riverside garden of Agra had acquired its typical form: the main architectural accent was shifted from the centre of the garden towards the riverfront, where the main buildings were arranged on

[35] Sarda, pp. 104–07.

[36] p. 121.

[37] Jahangir, ii, pp. 142, 150 f., 173 f.

[38] Crowe et al.; Bazmee Ansari 1960.

[39] Jahangir's India, pp. 2 ff.

[40] Koch 1986a.

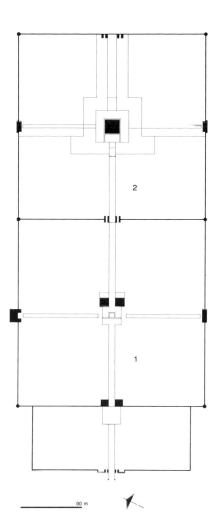

95 Kashmir,
Shalimar gardens,
founded 1620, site-
plan.
1 Bagh-i Farah
Bakhsh, 2 Bagh-i Fayz
Bakhsh.

80 m

96 Kashmir,
Shalimar gardens,
Farah Bakhsh,
platform in the
central pool connected
to the banks by two
bridgeways.
(Photo 1981)

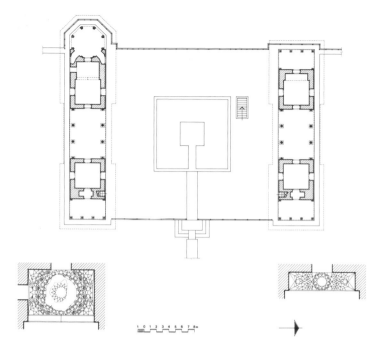

97 Agra, Ram Bagh
(Bagh-i Nur Afshan),
completed 1621, plan
of the riverside
terrace and its two
pavilions.

98 Agra, Ram Bagh
(Bagh-i Nur Afshan),
riverside terrace,
northern pavilion.
(Photo 1982)

a terrace. Thus they not only profited from the climate but also presented
a carefully composed riverside view framed by the corner towers of the
enclosure wall. In the Ram Bagh two oblong pavilions formed by open
verandahs (the Mughal *iwan*s) alternating with closed rooms (*hujra*s) flank
a pool on the riverside terrace. The scheme ingeniously transposes the concept of palatial *zanana* enclosures (fig. 94) into the lighter forms of freestanding garden architecture. The trabeate elements of the verandahs – multi-
faceted columns and capitals (probably painted originally with *muqarnas*)
and beams supported by voluted brackets, covered with white polished stucco (*chuna*) – anticipate early Shahjahani practice (pavilions at Ajmer (fig.

99 *Agra, Sikandra, Kanch Mahall, first quarter of 17th century. (Photo 1977)*

100 *Agra, Sikandra, Suraj Bhan ka Bagh, first quarter of 17th century, chini khana decoration of gate-pavilion. (Photo 1978)*

115); Shah Burj, Agra fort). However, they have a retrospective architectural decoration that echoes that of Lahore: peacock brackets, wall-paintings (partly after European models) and elaborate stucco vaults painted with birds and angels in the manner of the Kala Burj (pl. VIII).

Otherwise, the standard type for garden pavilions and villas remains the cube-shaped pavilion erected on variations of the *hasht bihisht* plan. A particularly elegant and well-preserved example with a delicate sandstone facing is the "Kanch Mahall" at Sikandra. Agra. Similar in style is the gatehouse of the "Suraj Bhan ka Bagh", also at Sikandra. It has a particularly elaborate *chini khana* decoration.[41]

[41] For plans and illus. see Smith 1901, chs. 4, 5.

The public works of Jahangir included the planting of trees along the highways from Agra to Attock and to Bengal, and the setting of monumental *kos minars* (milestones in the form of small towers) and wells along the road from Agra to Lahore.[42] In 1620 Jahangir ordered the construction of small stations (*ladhis*) along the route over the Pir Panjal pass into Kashmir.[43]

A number of *karwansara'i*s were built during his reign. Nur Jahan's Sara'i Nur Mahall in the Panjab (1028–30/1618–20) has an entrance-gate faced with sandstone, and carved — true to the fashion of the period — with animal, human and mythical figures similar to those appearing in tile-work on the outer wall of the Lahore fort.[44]

101 Sara'i Nur Mahall, 1028–30/ 1618–20, western gate, outer facade. (Photo 1979)

The other great female patron of architecture of this period, Jahangir's mother Maryam al-Zamani, also sponsored a remarkable public work, a *ba'oli* (step-well) near the old ᶜ*idgah* at Brahambad, Bayana. A marble inscription on its gate dates it in the seventh year of Jahangir's reign (1612); it was thus built at the same time as Maryam al-Zamani's mosque at Lahore. The *ba'oli* was considered by the English traveller Mundy to be "the best of this Kinde that I have yett seene, . . . a very costly and curious peece of worke".[45] The scheme consists of a gate, four flights of stairs leading down to the water-level, and a well-shaft at the farther end of the main axis, all constructed in the local red sandstone. The step-well was a type of water architecture that had been brought to its richest development in Gujarat.[46] Typical for the Mughal treatment of the *ba'oli* is the clear and rational approach concentrating on the main components of the architecture; nonfunctional elements are reduced to a minimum.

The architectural patronage of the great nobleman and general ᶜAbd al-Rahim Khan-i Khanan, who — if we are to believe his eulogists — "turned Hindustan into Iran", includes important works of civic architecture at Burhanpur. The town had become the headquarters of the Mughals after the

[42] Jahangir, ii, p. 100.

[43] Jahangir, ii, p. 178.

[44] Begley 1983, pp. 168–70.

[45] p. 101; see also Jahangir, ii, p. 64. I thank Iqtidar Alam Khan for kindly providing me with a plan of the so far unpublished building

[46] Jain-Neubauer

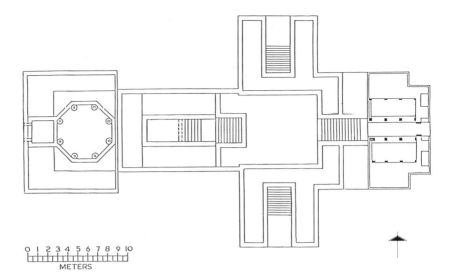

102   Bayana,
Brahambad, ba'oli of
Maryam al-Zamani,
plan. (Courtesy
I. A. Khan)

conquest of Khandesh, a region in west-central India, in 1601. Unique in India
are the still existing *qanat* works, an extensive irrigation system of underground waterpipes of Iranian inspiration (1024/1615). They served to bring
water from the foothills of the Satpura range to the town and to the Khan-i
Khanan's now lost Laᶜl Bagh. These artfully planned and cultivated gardens
with a large artifical lotus-pond in their middle became the great attraction
of Burhanpur, all the more so as the Khan-i Khanan threw them open to
the public (*khass-o-ᶜamm*) – a rare gesture of civic spirit for the times.[47]
Other works of urban architecture sponsored by the Khan-i Khanan during

103   Burhanpur,
public hammam
sponsored by ᶜAbd
al Rahim Khan-i
Khanan,
1016/1607 08,
ground-plan.

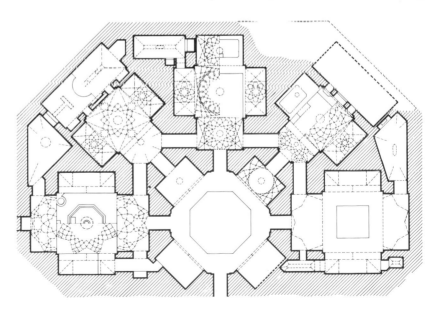

[47] Nahawandi, ii,
pp. 598 ff.; for the
later history of the
waterworks see *The
Imperial Gazetteer of
India*, ix: *Bomjur to
Central India*, p. 105.

his long tenure of Burhanpur were a *sara'i* (1027/1617–18) and a public *hammam* (1016/1607–08) near the fort. The *hammam* is noteworthy for its carefully thought-out plan and its elaborate vaults. Today the building has the plan of a truncated *muthamman baghdadi*; its ruined state does not allow us to determine whether this shape was intended or whether part of the building has disappeared. The full figure is based on the radial ninefold plan with two patterns of cross-axes (+ and x); the concept is close to the tomb of Anarkali at Lahore (fig. 87). The scheme is enriched by cruciform room compositions replacing the earlier simpler chambers, and by corridors linking the inner niches or arms of the cruciform units. They generate a square ambulatory around the central octagonal unit. Comparable configurations of rooms had already appeared in Akbari *hammams*;[48] new is that they are now organized according to a strictly geometrical scheme. The concept of the Burhanpur *hammam* is highlighted by the sophisticated plaster lining of the vaults; their different netted designs might almost be a pattern-book of Jahangiri vaulting. The supervisor, or perhaps even the architect, of this remarkable building was Muhammad ᶜAli, known as Gurg-i Khurasan.[49]

[48] For plans see Petruccioli 1988, fig. 131.

[49] Nahawandi, ii, p. 601; Naik, pp. 216–19.

Under Shah Jahan, Mughal architecture took on a new aesthetic and entered its classical phase. The architectural ideals of the period were symmetry and uniformity of shapes, governed by hierarchical accents.

The symmetrical planning of both individual buildings and large complexes became even more binding than in the previous periods. Compositions of bilateral symmetry on both sides of a central axis (*qarina*) were now given preference over centralized schemes.

Uniformity was achieved by the reduction of the architectural vocabulary to a few forms. The multi-faceted column with a *muqarnas* (or multi-faceted) capital and a cusped-arch base (base in the shape of an inverted cushion capital, whose four flat faces are outlined like a cusped arch) emerged as the chief columnar form. Although it had made its first appearance in Akbari architecture (Tan Sen's Baradari, fig. 48, Qush Khana, fig. 17, both Fatehpur Sikri) and was also used occasionally in Jahangir's period (Ram Bagh, or Bagh-i Nur Afshan, fig. 98), its widespread and consistent use in Shah Jahan's architecture entirely justifies the designation "Shahjahani column". In early Shahjahani architecture it was combined with one type of voluted bracket supporting architraves (pavilions at Ajmer, fig. 115; Shah Burj, Agra fort).[1] First in particularly distinguished buildings, later in a more general context, the Shahjahani column was often given a vegetal capital and/or base (figs. 137, 149). From about the early 1630s it was combined with a multi-cusped arch, another characteristic feature of the period (figs. 112, 122, 125).

The standardization of architecture also extended to the patterns of the vaults. Of the various experiments with decorative plaster vaults that were made in Jahangiri architecture, the network developed from points in concentric tiers was used almost exclusively. It gradually acquired the shape of a thin reticulated whorl pattern (*hammam* of the Red Fort of Delhi, fig. 132). Shah Jahan's authors now provide us with an architectural term for this type of work, namely *qalib kari* (mould-work); this indicates that the original plaster version of this type of vault was produced by means of moulds. The pattern was also applied in carved relief to the sandstone or marble facing of vaults (inner dome of the Taj Mahall).

The other main vault form of Shahjahani architecture was the coved ceiling (often with reticulated cavettos), which was particularly suitable for covering the now preferred rectangular halls (fig. 124).

Hierarchical and symbolical accents were set by means of an entirely new architectural vocabulary. Three-dimensionally modelled and decorated with revolutionary naturalistic plant motifs, it was destined to become archetypical for Indian architecture of the future. Its main elements were the "cypress-bodied" (*sarw-andam*) baluster column, the semicircular arch, and the curved roof (vault) or cornice (*bangla*).

The baluster column helps particularly well to show that these new forms owed their origin to a reawakened interest in synthesizing fresh sources. Before Shah Jahan, Mughal architects had already turned their attention to

[1] Koch 1982a, pp. 337 f.

104 Baldachin supported by baluster columns. From a title page by Lucas Cranach the Elder, 1531. Woodcut. (Based on A. F. Butsch, Handbook of Renaissance Ornament, 1878–80)

105 Eastern India, architectural frame supported by baluster columns standing on pots with overhanging leaves, 11th–12th centuries. London. British Museum, Bridge Collection, 1872, 7–1.48. (Photo 1979)

baluster-shaped columnar forms but, in the end, had refrained from fully accepting the characteristic bulb-shape. The elongated wooden baluster columns of the Transoxanian *iwan* (fig. 14) had inspired a stone column of Akbari architecture, which appears for instance in the east verandah of the Jahangiri Mahall in the Agra fort (fig. 39) or in the Rani ki Mahall of the Allahabad fort (fig. 53). The characteristic bulb at the bottom of the Transoxanian model was however omitted here, and a formally related pot-like element inserted instead in the lower part of the shaft.[2] The adaptation of the Transoxanian examples shows a first awareness of this particular columnar form. The actual shape of Shah Jahan's baluster column with its naturalistic acanthus decoration − taking the third dimension fully into account − was however derived from European sources, most likely prints of the Dürer circle, brought to the court by the Jesuits (Compare fig. 104 with figs. 122, 133). The characteristic combination of the column with an additional pot-like element at its foot − a *purna ghata* motif − was in turn inspired by a further source, namely the baluster columns of the Buddhist and Hindu architecture of eastern India (Compare fig. 105 with fig. 123). Since Akbar's days it had been an acknowledged region of influence for Mughal architecture.[3]

Eastern India also provided the models for the curved-up roof or vault, another characteristic element of the new Shahjahani vocabulary. Shah Jahan's authors term it *bangla* or *bangala* in allusion to its derivation from vernacular prototypes of Bengal (figs. 121, 133, 136).

[2] See above, pp. 40, 42, 55; and for this and the following see Koch 1982b.

[3] See Abu'l Fazl's remarks quoted above, p. 54.

[4] Koch 1982b and 1988b.

[5] Skelton.

[6] Fol. 18^v.

[7] Koch 1988b, n. 3.

[8] Wulff, pp. 92−97.

[9] Koch 1988b, n. 24; 1987b, pp. 39−44.

The baluster column, the semicircular arch and the *bangla* were — as symbols of rulership — at first strictly reserved for the architecture for formal appearances of the emperor (*jharokas*, baldachins, loggias).[4] They were expressed in white marble, which, together with very fine, highly polished white stucco from Gujarat (*chuna*), now became the favourite veneer of imperial buildings.

In a wider architectural context, other features quickly asserted themselves, in particular naturalistic flowery plant motifs derived from European herbals, which became the chief dado ornament of Shahjahani architecture.[5] On the whole, the use of plant motifs marked a reversion of architectural decoration from the figurative extravaganzas of the previous reign to artistic modes sanctioned by Islamic law, which became a matter of greater concern for Shah Jahan. At the same time, the flower and plant forms underlined the poets' assertion that the emperor's buildings were a paradise on earth, surpassing even the Qur'anic, mythical and natural models. The flowery motifs were executed in painting, (fig. 118) in sensuously carved relief-work in marble or stucco (*munabbat kari*, fig. 111), or in *parchin kari* (figs. 107, 110); the latter term describes the *commesso di pietre dure* technique, i. e. composite inlays of hard (= precious) stones.

This highly specialized technique of Florentine origin was soon mastered to such perfection by the lapidaries of Shah Jahan that the emperor's Persian historian Qazwini[6] (and after him many a modern author involved in the "*pietra dura* controversy")[7] considered it "a craft peculiar to the stonecutters of India" (*ṣanᶜat makhṣūṣ-i sangtarāshān-i Hindūstān*), while comparing it favourably to *khātam bandi*, the Iranian technique of inlays in wood.[8] The Mughal artisans were able to attain this high standard in the *commesso* technique because they were already skilled in the closely related, simpler stone intarsia technique.[9] The painterly effects that could be obtained with *commesso di pietre dure* made it possible to replace the earlier conventional stone intarsia patterns with the now favoured naturalistic motifs. The intention is made clear by the verses of Shah Jahan's court poet Abu Talib Kalim:

> "They have inlaid stone flowers in marble,
> Which surpass reality in colour if not in fragrance."[10]

Another innovation in interior decoration was the mosaic of mirror-pieces set in *chuna* (*ayina kari*, fig. 137).

The predilection for curvilinear forms also determined the profile of domes, which became increasingly more bulbous, possibly under the influence of Deccani architecture.[11]

A noteworthy new feature in religious and sepulchral architecture are multiple minarets. The practice, which was probably inspired by Ottoman examples, had announced itself with the quadruple minarets set on the gate of Akbar's tomb at Sikandra (fig. 68). From the formal point of view, multiple minarets were highly suitable for setting accents as compositional elements. From the semantic point of view, the frequent use of minarets as a symbol of Islam may be seen as an expression of Shah Jahan's more orthodox attitude towards religion.[12] Shahjahani minarets usually have a

[10] Eng. trans. in Begley and Desai, p. 83.

[11] Andrews 1985, p. 88.

[12] Burton-Page 1991b; Husain, pp. 100 f., 103 f., 187–89, et passim; Bloom, pp. 175 ff.

cylindrical or octagonal shaft surrounded by one or more balconies and topped by a *chhatri* (figs. 106, 140, pls. XII, XVII).

The planning of imperial building projects was done by the collective efforts of a court bureau of architects working under the emperor's close supervision — as Prince Khurram he had already shown himself to be "exceedingly fond of laying out gardens and founding buildings".[13] While the credit for these buildings, even for their overall concept, had to go to Shah Jahan as the supreme architect, his historians mention several of the men responsible for the actual realization. An outstanding figure in Shah Jahan's early reign was Mir ᶜAbd al-Karim, who had already literally made himself a name as Jahangir's leading architect. The most famous of the constructions he supervised — together with the noble Makramat Khan — was the Taj Mahall. Makramat Khan was later — when governor of Delhi — also employed as the final chief overseer of the construction of the Red Fort of Shahjahanabad, the emperor's palace-fortress in his new capital at Delhi. The only architects of Shah Jahan to whom the conventional term for this profession (*miᶜmar*) was applied were Ustad Ahmad Lahori and Ustad Hamid, who laid the foundations of the palace-fortress of Shahjahanabad. Ustad Ahmad is also reported to have been connected with the building of the Taj Mahall.[14]

Most of Shah Jahan's building projects were financed from the imperial purse. Recent research has shown that his building activities were by no means so great a burden on the treasury as some critics liked to make out.[15]

Where the emperor led the way, the court was bound to follow. The members of the imperial family and the great nobles of the court were in turn expected to respond to Shah Jahan's taste for architecture. Not only were they employed in imperial projects (Asaf Khan, ᶜAli Mardan Khan), but they were also encouraged and, at times, even ordered to sponsor buildings. Since often such structures would also be used by the emperor, they had to conform to his ideas. The emperor's daughter Jahanara fully shared her father's passion for building, thus culminating the Mughal tradition of female patronage of architecture that had been well represented by Jahangir's mother, Maryam al-Zamani, and his wife Nur Jahan. Not only the sponsoring but also the designing of buildings appears to have become a regular fashion at court, even affecting men of religion. Jahanara and the emperor's favourite son, Dara Shukoh, started a small architectural workshop at Kashmir under the guidance of their spiritual teacher, the Sufi mystic Mulla Shah Badakhshi.[16]

That Shah Jahan's reign was an era of great architectural awareness is also reflected in the contemporary sources. From no other Mughal period do we possess such detailed comments on architecture. By inference and analogy, these also shed light on Mughal architectural phenomena of earlier or later periods that are not explained in the literature. Shahjahani texts also provide the broadest basis for the understanding of Mughal architectural terminology.

[13] Kanbo, i, p. 108.

[14] Lutf Allah Muhandis, *Diwan*, Eng. trans. in Chaghtai 1937, pp. 202 f.; see also Begley 1982; and Qaisar, pp. 8 ff.

[15] Moosvi

[16] See below, p. 117.

[17] Kanbo, i, pp. 11 f.

Following the usual custom, Shah Jahan, after his accession, built the tomb of his father at Lahore in one of the gardens on the far side of the river Ravi (1037–47/1628–38). In Jahangir's tomb the classical *char bagh* layout was combined with a *chauk-i jilau khana* (ceremonial forecourt or square), which also contained a mosque. The peculiar shape of the mausoleum was dictated by Jahangir's wish to be buried under the open sky, like his ancestor Babur; consequently a tombstone (*marqad*) was set on a platform (*chabutra*), which in turn was placed on a monumental podium (*takhtgah*) with corner minarets.[17] The scheme is clearly indebted to the tradition of the platform tombs of the previous reign, for which Shah Jahan's authors provide us in

106 Lahore, Shahdara, tomb of Jahangir, 1628–38. (Photo 1979)

107 Lahore, Shahdara, tomb of Jahangir, tombstone in the sepulchral chamber in the monumental platform. (Photo 1979)

retrospect with the technical term *takhtgah* (tomb). The podium is faced with sandstone (from Fatehpur) inlaid with stone; the tombstone (not preserved) showed one of the first instances of true *commesso di pietre dure*, representing naturalistic flowers inlaid in marble. An idea of it can be obtained from the tombstone in the lower tomb-chamber.[18]

The design of Jahangir's tomb was repeated only once, on about half the scale and without corner minarets, in the tomb of Nur Jahan (d. 1055/1645), built by Jahangir's widow herself nearby.[19]

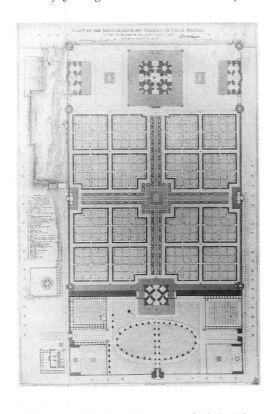

108 Site-plan of the tomb garden of the Taj Mahall and the forecourt with its flanking subsidiary structures, by Col. J. A. Hodgson, 1828. (Photo British Library [India Office Library and Records], London).

The sepulchral architecture of Shah Jahan, and indeed of the Mughals, culminates in the famous mausoleum of Shah Jahan's favourite wife Arjumand Banu Begam at Agra (1041–52/1632–43; pl. XVII).[20] The tomb derived its name from her title Mumtaz Mahall, distorted by popular etymology to Taj Mahall. Comparable to some extent to Ottoman schemes, the tomb garden forms part of a larger, carefully planned complex; it is preceded on its southern side by a *chauk-i jilau khana* – a feature that had already been introduced in Jahangir's tomb. The *jilau khana* square is framed on both sides by smaller residential courts for the tomb attendants (*khawasspuras*), bazaar streets and subsidiary tomb enclosures. Further south[21] followed a complex divided by two intersecting bazaar streets (*char su bazar*) into four (*karwan*)*sara'i*s; still further south was a square (*chauk*) with another bazaar and two more *sara'i*s. The surrounding area had by the time of the completion of the tomb developed into a regular township named Mumtazabad, now known as Tajganj. The income of the bazaars and the *karwansara'is* –

[18] Thompson.

[19] M. W. U. Khan, pp. 58–60.

[20] For a recent bibliography see Pal et al.; and Begley and Desai.

109 *Taj Mahall,*
section.

together with that of thirty villages from the district of Agra — was devoted by imperial command to the upkeep of the mausoleum.[22]

In its layout, the garden is a typical Agra riverside garden on a monumental scale, with a raised terrace (on which are placed the main buildings) combined with a lower *char bagh*. At about the same time, Shah Jahan's architects realized a comparable scheme in the residential courtyard of the Anguri Bagh in the Agra fort (figs. 36/5, 121); thus, the plan of the Taj garden represents just another — albeit grander — instance of interchangeable ideas in the funerary and secular architecture of the Mughals. That a typical plan of Mughal residential architecture was used as a setting for the tomb indicates that it was meant to represent an earthly replica of one of the houses of the heavenly Paradise, rather than — as has recently been speculated — an embodiment of complex concepts of Islamic cosmology.[23]

True to the architectural ideal of the period, the whole scheme is founded on strict bilateral symmetry with emphasis on the features on the central axis: the grandiose group of the tomb (*rauza*) and its four minarets flanked by a mosque and an assembly-hall (*mihman khana*) set the main accent. Radial symmetry is observed in the gatehouse and the tomb proper, both of which follow the ninefold plan. That of the tomb is inscribed in a *muthamman baghdadi* and is derived from the earlier radially planned variants of the model (tomb of Humayun, fig. 19, Todar Mal's Baradari, fig. 24; tomb of Anarkali, fig. 87). The plan of the Taj Mahall uses particularly those elements — including the square ambulatory around the central octagon introduced in the Burhanpur *hammam* (fig. 103), — that lend themselves to perfect balance of composition. Some of the earlier solutions

[21] Not on J. A. Hodgson's plan because only surviving in fragments, but appearing on eighteenth-century plans, see Pal et al., fig. 41; for a reconstructed plan see Begley and Desai, fig. 17.

[22] Lahori, ii, pp. 322–30; Kanbo, ii, pp. 315–20; for new trans. and illus. see Begley and Desai, pp. 65 ff.

[23] Begley 1979.

(tomb of Humayun, tomb of Anarkali) may be more creative and original – that of the Taj Mahall is certainly the most harmonious.

The elevation of the tomb – composed of *pishtaqs* flanked by double-storey niches – brings the cubical tomb of the Delhi type enhanced by Deccani features (bulbous profile of the dome) to a formal apotheosis of unparalleled elegance and harmony. The balanced proportions are highlighted by the sophisticated facing of the brick structure: the white marble inlaid with *pietre dure* reacts to atmospheric changes and enhances the mystical and mythical aura of the building.

The question whether a European architect was responsible for the design of the mausoleum much occupied Western scholars of an earlier day, who preferred to ascribe the unique qualities of the Taj to European rather than Asian genius.[24] Since the mausoleum is entirely within the stream of Mughal architecture, the possible involvement of a European architect appears to be of rather secondary importance. If the Italian goldsmith Geronimo Veroneo was indeed consulted in the planning, it was only as one of a larger team directed by Shah Jahan. Tangible evidence for European in-

110 Taj Mahall, tombstone of Mumtaz Mahall inscribed with the date of her death (1041/1631); behind, tombstone of Shah Jahan, added in 1076/1666. (Photo 1981)

111 Taj Mahall, dado with flowery plants from one of the outer niches. (Photo 1978)

fluence on the Taj Mahall is confined to the architectural decoration, to the exquisite *pietre dure* inlay and the sensuously carved flowers and vases of the dados (*izara*). All the subsidiary structures of the Taj complex are faced with red sandstone; special features, such as domes, may be clad in white marble. The lesser tombs have the form of single-storey regular octagons surrounded either by pillared verandahs or by eight *pishtaq*s of equal size (pl. XIV). Both versions are surmounted by pronounced bulbous domes.

The pillared version appears in the tombs of Satti al-Nisa Khanum (d. 1056/1647, now generally identified as that in the southwest corner of the *jilau khana*), of "Sirhindi Begam" (in the southeast corner of the *jilau khana*), and in an unidentified tomb outside the east wall of the Taj complex. This tomb type is of particular interest as it suddenly revives an earlier form that had been the most distinct sepulchral type of Delhi Sultanate architecture. The prototype, displaying the chunky articulation of the Tughluq style, was the tomb of Khan-i Jahan Maqbul Tilangani in Nizamuddin (c. 1368),[25] which had several epigons in Sayyid, Lodi and Suri architecture (fig. 34). After being used once in early Mughal architecture for the tomb of Adham Khan at Mehrauli (d. 969/1562, fig. 35),[26] the type fell into disuse in sepulchral architecture. It emerged, however, transformed into a light trabeate form (in which a *chhatri* may replace the funerary dome), in residential architecture, in which context some examples have already been noted, namely the Qush Khana (without topping *chhatri* or dome) at Fatehpur Sikri (fig. 17), the topmost storey of the Chalis Sutun of the Allahabad fort (fig. 55), and the Shah Burj in the Agra fort (completed 1637, fig. XIII). With the subsidiary tombs of the Taj complex the type reappears in sepulchral architecture, still with the delicate articulation of the verandah. Each of the faces has three arcades with cusped arches and Shahjahani columns. This tomb form was not used again in Mughal architecture.

[24] Havell 1903; Hosten. For a recent discussion of this approach see Metcalf, pp. 46–48.

[25] Welch and Crane, fig. 7.

[26] Zafar Hasan 1915–22, iii, 1920, p. 82.

A massive version of the subsidiary tombs, showing in each of its eight faces a *pishtaq* with a deep arched niche, is represented by the tomb of "Fatehpuri Begam" outside the western wall of the *chauk-i jilau khana* (fig. XIV). This form also appears in other sepulchral buildings of the period. Particularly close is the tomb of Asaf Khan (d. 1051/1641) at Lahore; the tomb of ᶜAli Mardan Khan (c. 1650), also at Lahore, has a different dome, shaped on models of earlier Mughal architecture (tomb of Humayun) – both tombs have been stripped of their original veneer.[27] Also a regular octagon, but with a less bold elevation, is the marble-faced tomb of "Shaykh Chilli" at Thanesar north of Panipat and Karnal.[28] The surrounding *chhajjas* topping the main body of the structure and its rather shallow niches bring the concept close to that of the earlier tomb of Firuz Khan at Agra, dating from Jahangir's period (fig. 72). The overall concept also conforms to the tradition of the Jahangiri platform tombs, here integrated into a large, four-winged complex.

The Gujarat-derived tomb with an inner domed chamber and a surrounding square verandah – which is structurally closely related to the pillared version of the octagonal tomb – served as a pattern for the reconstruction of the *rauza* of Shaykh Nizam al-Din Auliya, the famous Chishti saint of Delhi. The work was sponsored by Khalil Allah Khan, governor of Delhi, in 1063/1652–53, and consists of a marble verandah of multi-lobed arches and baluster columns built in four straight walks around the old tomb-chamber. Above it rises a pronounced bulbous dome.[29] The construction illustrates very clearly how conventional Mughal building types were reinterpreted by means of the new organic vocabulary.

Among the square tombs of the period may be mentioned the "Chini ka Rauza" on the east bank of the Jamna at Agra. On the Jaipur plan it is inscribed as Rauza of Afzal Khan (actually spelled "Rauja Afjal Khã", fig. 3/3), which confirms the local tradition attributing this tomb to ᶜAllami Afzal Khan Shirazi (d. 1048/1639), *diwan-i kul* (minister in charge of imperial finance) of Shah Jahan.[30] The tomb derives its popular name from its severely damaged and now heavily restored outer facing with tile mosaic in the Lahore style, a truly exotic element in the sepulchral architecture of Agra. The structure is raised on a classical square *hasht bihisht* plan with

[27] M. W. U. Khan, pp. 57, 63.

[28] Parihar, pp. 35 f., pl. 36.

[29] Zafar Hasan 1922, p. 13.

[30] Shah Nawaz Khan, i, 149–53.

[31] Smith 1901, pp. 3–17, pls. 7–57.

[32] M. W. U. Khan, p. 67.

[33] For the date see Koch 1982a, p. 337, n. 18.

pishtaqs in the centre of each elevation. It has elaborate painted vaults;[31] the main dome is lined with concentric tiers of arched *muqarnas*, a retrospective feature still indebted to the experimental vaults of Jahangir's period.

A less successful specimen of a square tomb on a ninefold plan is the tomb of Da'i Anga, Shah Jahan's wetnurse (d. 1082/1671–72), at Lahore.[32] It is faced with plaster and tile mosaic, which at Lahore is of course a conventional feature. The low and wide proportions of the main body of the building and the *chhatris* over each corner rather give it the appearance of a Jahangiri *takhtgah* tomb, on which the massive central dome seems an aberration.

Palaces

Another keynote of Shah Jahan's architectural patronage was palace and garden architecture. He had the palace in the fort of Agra reconstructed, made changes to the fort of Lahore and built a fortress-palace in his newly founded city at Delhi, appropriately named Shahjahanabad.

Shah Jahan also commissioned several pleasure houses. In 1046/1636 he completed the group of white marble pavilions on the bank of the Ana Sagar lake at Ajmer that had been begun "in a fresh style" under Jahangir.[33] The pavilions vary the theme of the flat-roofed hypostyle hall in an almost entirely trabeate idiom consisting of Shahjahani columns supporting voluted brackets, architraves and a flat roof set off by an ornamental parapet. The whole architecture breathes the pure classical spirit for which Shahjahani buildings became celebrated. However, the fact that the complex was partly constructed by Jahangir shows – like the topmost storey of Akbar's tomb, the Agra buildings of Nur Jahan (Bagh-i Nur Afshan, tomb of I'timad al-Daula) or the Chaunsath Khamba at Nizamuddin, Delhi – that the basis for this new marble style was laid firmly in the previous reign.

Shah Jahan's building programme also included several hunting-palaces, which have largely been ignored in the literature. Outstanding are his large

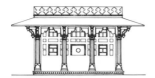
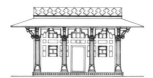

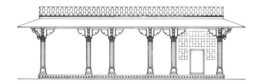

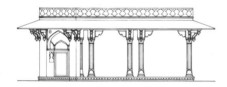

115 Ajmer, pavilions built by Jahangir and Shah Jahan on the bank of the Ana Sagar lake, completed 1636, elevations.

116 Ajmer, Ana Sagar, pavilion 4, landward facade. (Photo 1985)

complexes at Bari and Rup Bas, built entirely in red sandstone (completed 1046/1637). Contrary to the great urban palaces, they are almost completely preserved, and thus show the full scheme of a Shahjahani palace, from the halls and pavilions for the court ceremonial to the retainers' quarters and sanitary installations.[34] Another of his hunting-palaces, now almost entirely destroyed, was that of Palam (actually in the village Hashtsal) near Delhi (completed 1634). Its most outstanding surviving feature is a hunting-tower, popularly known as Hashtsal Minar, built in emulation of the practice of

[34] Koch, *The Hunting Palaces of Shah Jahan*, forthcoming.

[35] Koch 1991a.

117 Bari, Lal Mahall, main complex, completed 1637. Lake front. (Photo 1982)

118 Bari, Lal Mahall, main complex, hammam of the emperor with wall-paintings. (Photo 1978)

119 Bari, Lal Mahall, main complex, latrines of the female quarters. (Photo 1982)

Akbar and Jahangir. It is not decorated with hunting-trophies like its forerunners but — an interesting instance of revivalist architecture — its surface copies that of the lowest storey of the famous Qutb Minar at Delhi, which was built between the end of the twelfth and the beginning of the thirteenth century as a visible sign of the establishment of Muslim rule in northern India (pl. II).[35]

The Red Fort of Agra presents us with the first official palace architecture of Shah Jahan. The nucleus of his reconstruction (1037–46/1628–37) consists of a complex of three courts. The east wing of the great courtyard with the hall of public audiences forms the western portion of two smaller courts, both facing the river Jamna, the "Anguri Bagh" ("Grape-Garden") and the "Machchhi Bhawan" ("Fish-House") (pl. XIII, fig. 36). All three courtyards are organized in a similar way and follow the scheme of the riverside garden of Agra: three of their sides are formed by narrow wings of one or two storeys; on the fourth, the eastern side, arranged on terraces, are the individual structures for the main ceremonial functions of the court and for the personal use of the emperor and his daughter Jahanara. This courtyard pattern – dictated by a preference for riverside sites – was to remain the chief compositional element of the palace architecture of Shah Jahan. In the Anguri Bagh the riverside buildings („Khass Mahall") consist of the emperor's sleeping-pavilion (Aramgah) flanked to the north by the pavilion where he appeared to his subjects (Bangla-i Darshan), which is followed by the Shah Burj ("Royal Tower"), used for private counselling. To the south of the Aramgah is the Bangla of Jahanara, which formed part of her apartments in the adjoining part of the south wing of the court. The three courtyard wings contain residential quarters for the women. In the Machchhi Bhawan the buildings on the riverside terrace consist of the hall of private audiences (Daulat Khana-i Khass, earlier termed *ghusl khana*, popularly call-

Fortress-palaces

121 Agra fort, Anguri Bagh and the Khass Mahall, consisting of the Aramgah flanked on the left by the Bangla i Darshan and on the right by the Bangla-i Jahanara; completed 1637. (Photo 1979)

122 Agra fort, Diwan-i Khass and south wing of the Machchhi Bhawan with imperial baldachin projecting from the centre, completed 1637. (Photo 1979)

ed Diwan-i Khass) and, opposite, the Hammam, stripped by the English in the nineteenth century of its marble porch and of its revetments and paving.[36] Below, on the ground floor, were vaulted rooms housing the treasury. The courtyard wings contained offices behind arcaded galleries. Projecting from the centre of the southern wing is a baldachined marble seat for the emperor; its baluster colums and semicircular arches with rich naturalistic plant decoration are in studied contrast to the repeated monotony of the Shahjahani columns and multi-lobed arches of the surrounding arcades.[37]

The main individual pavilions, the Aramgah and Diwan-i Khass, elaborate and expand on the favourite Mughal pavilion theme of the combination of an inner hall (now termed *tanabi khana* or *tambi khana*) with a pillared porch or verandah (the Mughal *iwan*). The execution is enhanced by the marble facing. New in the palatial building programme is the great hall of public audiences, the Daulat Khana-i Khass-o-ᶜAmm, or Chihil Sutun

[36] Koch 1982a.
[37] Koch 1982b.

123 *Agra fort, south wing of Machchhi Bhawan, baluster column of the imperial baldachin. (Photo 1979)*

124 *Agra fort, Diwan-i Khass, inner hall. (Photo 1979)*

("Forty-pillared Hall"),[38] popularly known as the Diwan-i ᶜAmm. The flat-roofed hypostyle construction is erected on a grid pattern. Its bays are demarcated by coved ceilings set off by cusped arches and large Shahjahani columns, paired on the outer sides. The design is evolved from forerunners in the funerary and mosque architecture of Jahangir's reign. The overall concept, in particular the deployment of paired pillars around the periphery, closely relates the audience-hall to the Chaunsath Khamba at Nizamuddin,

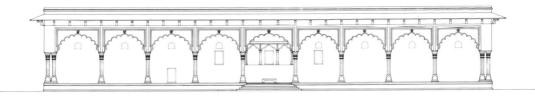

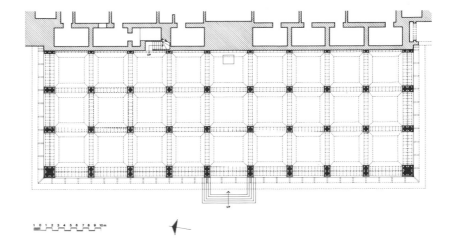

*125 Agra fort,
Diwan-i ʿAmm hall,
elevation.*

*126 Agra fort,
Diwan-i ʿAmm hall,
plan.*

³⁸ "Forty" is used
in the sense of
"many"; the hall
actually has forty-
eight freestanding
columns and twelve
half-columns.

³⁹ For an addi-
tional discussion of
the individual
buildings and for
literature see An-
drews 1986b.

⁴⁰ ʿInayat Khan,
Eng. trans. pp. 406 f.;
Sanderson 1914;
Andrews 1986b; for a
pre-Mutiny plan see
Petruccioli 1985; for a
pre-Mutiny
panorama by the
Delhi artist Mazhar
Ali Khan see Pal et
al., fig. 252.

which is however square and has no fixed orientation (fig. 89). The Agra
Diwan-i ʿAmm, on the other hand, has an oblong shape that generates three
aisles along the longer side and nine naves along the shorter side. This plan
has its closest parallel in the Patthar Masjid at Srinagar, which is however
built in a more massive idiom with cruciform piers instead of columns
(fig. 91). Both buildings have a wider nave in the centre indicating the direction in which the hall should be read. In the case of the mosque it leads to
the *mihrab*, in the case of the audience-hall to the emperor's place of appearance, described with the Sanskrit term *jharoka*. Such parallels were by
no means accidental: Shah Jahan's eulogists extol the emperor as the *qibla*
and *mihrab* – the direction of prayer – of his subjects. The Mughal
emperor's aspiration to unite both spiritual and political authority could not
be given a more explicit architectural expression. The reference is reinforced
by a mosque integrated in the centre of the western wing of the courtyard
– exactly opposite the audience hall (fig. 36/3).³⁹ The audience-hall of Agra
served as a model for those in the palaces of Lahore and Shahjahanabad.

The ideas of Agra were pressed into a rigid formal scheme in the Red Fort
of Delhi, the fortress-palace (*qilʿa*) of Shahjahanabad (1048–58/1639–48).⁴⁰
Since it was a new foundation, the Shahjahani ideal of bilateral symmetry
could be realized almost unimpeded by earlier structures. The plan has the
form of a giant oblong *muthamman baghdadi*. After I was permitted in 1984
to measure the entire enclosure wall it was possible for the first time to

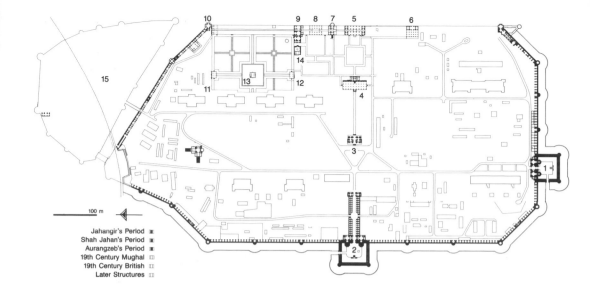

reconstruct the modular plan.[41] It was based on the unit of the Shahjahani yard, called *gaz* or *zira*[c], of 0.81–0.82 m. The two longer sides of the *muthamman baghdadi* measure c. 656 m, the two shorter sides c. 328 m, and the chamfering of the four corners c. 116 m. Hence it is evident that the plan was generated by means of a grid of squares, each square with a side of 82 m, or a hundred *gaz*. The longer sides of the grid thus consisted of ten squares (= 820 m), the shorter sides of six squares (= 492 m), of which eight squares were used for the longer sides of the *muthamman*, four squares for the shorter sides, and the diagonal of one square for each of the four corner chamfers. In the execution, however, practical concerns outweighed the ideals of perfect geometrical planning, and the figure was extended in the northeast by a wedge to accommodate the small fort of Salimgarh (Jahangir's Nurgarh) within the lines of defence.

127 Delhi, Shahjahanabad, Red Fort, 1048–58/1639–48, ground-plan of its present state. 1 Delhi Darwaza, 2 Lahori Darwaza with covered bazaar, 3 Naqqar Khana, 4 Hall of Diwan-i ʿAmm, 5 Rang Mahall, 6 Moti Mahall, 7 Aramgah, 8 Diwan-i Khass, 9 Hammam, 10 Shah Burj, 11 Sawan, 12 Bhadon, 13 Zafar Mahall, 14 Moti Masjid, 15 Salimgarh.

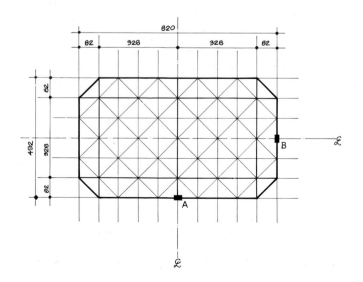

128 Delhi, Red Fort, construction-scheme.

The pavilions and halls for the emperor and the *zanana* were threaded along a canal, the Nahr-i Bihisht ("River of Paradise"), along the riverfront. This semiofficial and private axis was met at a right-angle by the public axis: the great courtyard of public audiences, preceded by the Jilau Khana, into which abuts a covered bazaar providing through the Lahori Gate at its western end the main access to the palace. Through the centre of the Jilau Khana, parallel to the riverfront, was laid another axis, along which were set the imperial stables and an open bazaar street. It was entered through the second main gate, the Delhi Darwaza.

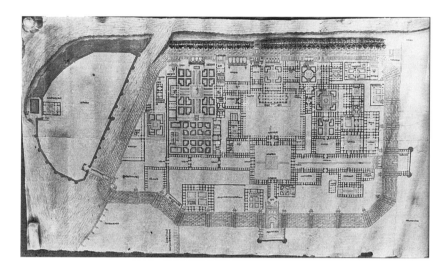

Today, only the enclosure wall and the principal buildings remain divorced from their original context. Their architecture is evolved from that of the pavilions and halls of the Agra fort. As at Agra, contemporary descriptions inform us in detail about the designation and function of the main buildings (fig. 127). The Naqqar Khan ("Drum-House") provided access to the court-yard of *khass-o-ʿamm*. Sited on the same axis is the hall of the Daulat Khana-i Khass-o-ʿAmm, or Chihil Sutun, closely modelled on its earlier counter-part at Agra. Its central wider nave leads to the emperor's throne-*jharoka* in the form of a marble *bangla* supported by four baluster columns set before an arched niche in the back wall of the hall. The niche is decorated with Florentine *pietre dure* panels and corresponding Mughal work, showing — besides plant and flower motifs — birds and also small lions at the foot of the wall — the only place in the whole palace where animated beings are depicted. This infringement of the Islamic ban on depictions (unusual for Shah Jahan, particularly in the public sphere) was justified by the conception of the whole composition as a copy of the throne of Solomon, the Qur'anic prophet-king and ideal ruler in Islamic thinking. The symbolism was rein-forced by a panel inserted in the top of the wall of the throne-niche, showing Orpheus playing to the beasts (pl. XVI). The decontextualized Florentine image was meant to symbolize the ideal rule of Shah Jahan, whose justice — like that of Solomon or Kayumarth, the first mythical king of Iran — would make the lion lie down with the lamb and, in the human world, free

[41] The reconstruc-tion has been work-ed out by Richard A. Barraud.

the oppressed from their oppressors.[42] Such associations are characteristic
for the selection and reception of European art at the Mughal court.

Further on, still on the same axis as the Diwan-i ᶜAmm hall and overlooking the river, is the ᶜImtiyaz or Rang Mahall ("Palace of Distinction"
or "Colourful Palace"), which was the main *zanana* building. The "Moti
Mahall" ("Pearl Mansion") to its south, now the Fort Museum, also belongs
to the *zanana*. North of the Rang Mahall are the buildings of the emperor
(the Aramgah) and the less official court buildings (the Daulat Khana-i Khass
or Diwan-i Khass, the Hammam and the Shah Burj). Also preserved are two
pavilions in the palace gardens, popularly named "Bhadon" and "Sawan"

[42] Discussed in
detail by Koch 1988b.

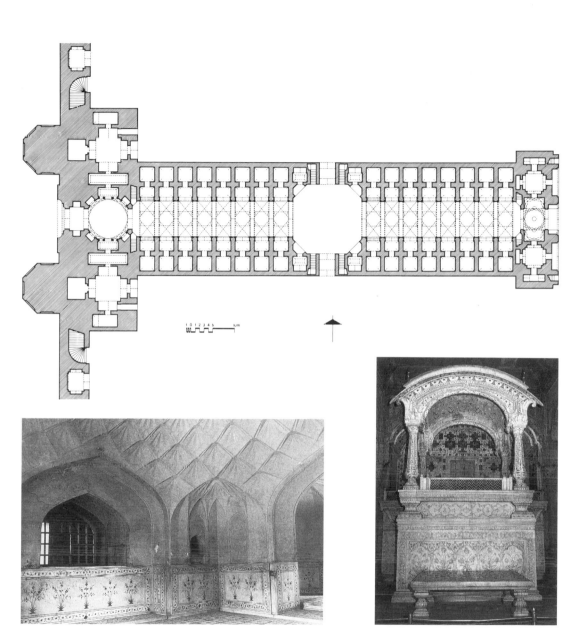

131 Delhi, Red Fort, covered bazaar, ground-plan.

132 Delhi, Red Fort, Hammam, interior. (Photo 1979)

133 Delhi, Red Fort, Diwan-i ᶜAmm, throne-jharoka. (Photo 1979)

after the Hindi months of the rainy season. They have the shape of simple halls, whose multi-lobed arches are supported by baluster columns. This shows that the new three-dimensional organic style was by now employed in a wider context. One pavilion is the mirror image of the other − a perfect example of the formal ideal *qarina*.

The public east-west axis of the fortress-palace is extended via the Lahori Gate into the city by the Chandni Chauk, a bazaar street abutting in the Fatehpuri Masjid. The main north-south axis is continued via the Delhi Gate by the Fayz Bazaar. These, together with the construction of the Jamiᶜ Masjid opposite the fort (pl. XII), were the main planning accents, the town being built by infill. The members of Shah Jahan's family and his nobles

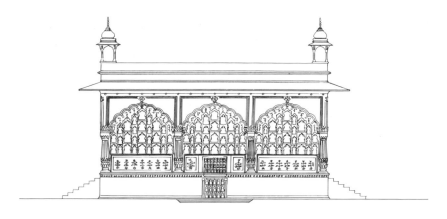

SCALE IN METRES

*134 Delhi, Red Fort,
Bhadon, elevation.
(After Archaeological
Survey of India)*

*135 Delhi, Red Fort,
Bhadon pavilion.
(Photo 1978)*

were encouraged (also by financial assistance) to build their *hawelis* (courtyard houses) in the new city. Outstanding here was the complex of Jahanara
in the Chandni Chauk, consisting of a *sara'i*, a *hammam* and her garden
Sahibabad.[43]

Shah Jahan's additions to the fort of Lahore are confined to the reconstruction of individual buildings in the years between 1628 and 1634, and in
1645.[44] In 1628 he ordered the building of the great hall of the Diwan-i
ᶜAmm (now greatly altered) on the pattern of that of Agra.[45] At the same
time, he also rebuilt the Shah Burj, which had been begun under Jahangir
(fig. 93/8 and 3). The work was completed by ᶜAbd al-Karim under the
superintendence of Wazir Khan in 1041/1631–32. The Shah Burj of Lahore
has not the form of a tower like its counterparts at Agra and Delhi but that
of the three-sided block projecting from the north front of the fort. This

[43] Kanbo, iii,
pp. 37 ff.; Blake,
pp. 158 ff.; Petruccioli
and Terranova 1985;
Burton-Page 1965a.

[44] Nur Bakhsh
1902–03; Andrews
1986a

[45] Sanderson
1909–10, who also
publishes a ground-
plan of the hall
(fig. 1).

[46] Lahori, ii,
p. 414.

block forms the northern wing of a large courtyard, which occupies the northwestern corner of the palace. While the outer fronts still conform to the decorative facing of Jahangir, in the interior we find typical Shahjahani innovations: the halls are decorated with the new mirror mosaic (*ayina kari*). In the west wing of the court is a pavilion with the new *bangla* shape. Today called "Naulakha", it conforms to the four-sided *chauchala* type of *bangla*.

In 1043/1634 Shah Jahan ordered further alterations to the palace of Lahore, which affected the Ghusl Khana (Daulat Khana-i Khass) and the Khwabgah. The last of Shah Jahan's additions to the fort of Lahore took place in 1055/1645 and consisted of a "building entirely of marble overlooking the river".[46] The description matches the marble hall today described as Shah Jahan's Diwan-i Khass (fig. 93/5).

136 Lahore fort,
Naulakha pavilion,
completed 1631–32.
(Photo 1979)

137 Lahore fort,
Shah Burj, completed
1041/1631–32, main
hall decorated with
ayina kari.
(Photo 1979)

Among Shah Jahan's important garden constructions is an addition to the Shalimar gardens near Srinagar in Kashmir in the form of another *char bagh* named Fayz Bakhsh ("Bounty-bestowing") (1043/1634) to the northeast of the earlier Farah Bakhsh (fig. 95/2). Its central feature is a pavilion in the local dark grey stone standing in a pool with fountains.[47]

138 Kashmir, Shalimar gardens, pavilion in centre of Bagh-i Fayz Bakhsh, 1634. (Photo 1981)

Shah Jahan's main garden foundation was the Bagh-i Fayz Bakhsh wa Farah Bakhsh, or Shalimar gardens, at Lahore (1051–52/1641–42; pl. XV), inspired by its namesake at Kashmir (and later imitated by its namesake at Delhi). The earlier Kashmir scheme of two terraced *char bagh*s enthreaded on a central waterway is enriched at Lahore by a rectangular terrace inserted between them. The water-supply was provided by a canal, the construction of which was organized by the Persian noble ᶜAli Mardan Khan, who had defected to the Mughal court in 1638.[48] His knowledge of architecture and engineering made him a welcome addition to Shah Jahan's architectural council.

Of particular interest among the numerous, now largely lost nonimperial gardens are the Nishat Bagh and the "Peri Mahall" in Kashmir. The Nishat Bagh ("Garden of Gladness") situated on the bank of the Dal lake was founded by another gentleman-architect of the period, the great noble Yamin al-Daula Asaf Khan, Shah Jahan's father-in-law. He was not only a noted patron of architecture but also himself "well versed in the subtleties of this craft (*sanᶜat*)".[49] In this capacity he was employed in the planning and realization of imperial building enterprises. In Asaf Khan's Nishat Bagh the Mughal garden of Kashmir is given an unprecedented monumental scale by extending it to twelve terraces. The court authors of Shah Jahan are full of its praise and go so far as to rate it next to the emperor's own Shalimar Garden.

The Peri Mahall ("Fairies' Palace") is based on a comparable design, but its seven stepped terraces are higher and more compact. The fronts of the terraces are faced with single- or double-storey arcades projecting forward in the centre; the corners of the lower terraces are fortified by octagonal towers.

[47] For sketch plans and illus. of this and the following see Crowe et al.

[48] ᶜInayat Khan, pp. 262, 277, 298.

[49] Lahori, i/1, p. 224.

[50] Muhammad Bakhtawar Khan, ii, p. 410.

[51] ᶜInayat Khan, p. 458.

[52] Abu Talib Kalim, *Diwan*, pp. 346–51; partly trans. Koch 1986b.

139 *Kashmir, Peri Mahall, second quarter of 17th century. (Photo 1981)*

The scheme is more architecturalized than any other Kashmir garden and, in the manner of a "hanging garden", substructure and plantation contribute equally to the composition. The foundation of the Peri Mahall is associated by tradition with Shah Jahan's son Dara Shukoh and his spiritual guide Mulla Shah Badakhshi, or Akhnun Mulla Shah. It appears to belong to those "lofty buildings, spirit-increasing dwellings and heart-attracting recreation places" which the saint designed and constructed with the support of the prince and his sister Jahanara.[50] These architectural creations also include a mosque and its subsidiary buildings (completed 1061/1651),[51] as well as a *hammam* (1059/1649–50) on the Hari Parbat hill at Srinagar, all constructed in the local dark grey stone.

At Agra, the most notable garden of Shah Jahan's reign was the Bagh-i Jahanara, now known by its corrupted name Zahara Bagh (fig. 3/2). It is situated south of the Bagh-i Nur Afshan or Ram Bagh and, although largely destroyed, presents enough evidence to show that it conformed to the tradition of the riverside gardens of Agra. Parts of the riverside terrace and one of its framing towers (the southern) are still visible today. The garden is of particular historical interest because it was not founded by Babur or one of his daughters, as generally assumed, but by Shah Jahan's wife Mumtaz Mahall. It is the only architectural project known to have been sponsored by her. After her death it passed to her daughter Jahanara, who had it renovated and – if we are to believe the contemporary eulogists – turned it into the most splendid garden of Agra.[52]

Mosques

Shah Jahan's enormous building programme also encompassed a considerable number of mosques – his was in fact the golden age of Mughal mosque construction. Shah Jahan, who liked to be seen as a renewer (*mujaddid*) of Islam, commissioned or initiated the construction of more mosques than any other Mughal ruler before him. In the mosque architecture of this period we can discern two main types, which had already become distinct in Jahangiri architecture. The first, with massive *pishtaq*ed prayer-halls surmounted by either three or five domes, is used most conspicuously for the great city mosques, the *jami^c masjids*; it may also be equipped with multiple

minarets. The second, lighter type is based on the additive grid system of
vaulted bays, and may appear without *pishtaq* and outer domes; it has no
minarets. This form was preferred for smaller mosques with a special imperial connotation.

The series of great city mosques is initiated by that of Wazir Khan at
Lahore,[53] of local brick and tile construction, and that of Jahanara at Agra
in red sandstone highlighted with white marble. Like the great Tughluq mosques in Delhi or the Jami꜀ Masjid at Fatehpur Sikri, they are elevated above
their surroundings on a podium. The great courtyard is enclosed by narrow
wings.

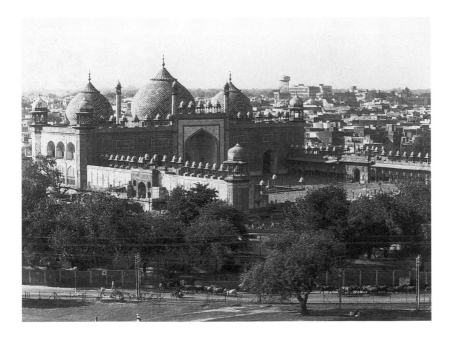

In the mosque of Wazir Khan (1044/1634–35), the wings consist of unconnected *hujras* interrupted by three axial gateways. New are the four minarets in the corners of the court. The prayer-hall (accentuated by a high *pishtaq*) rises above the level of the courtyard wings and follows the pattern of the one-aisle, five-bay type of Delhi mosque (which at Lahore had earlier found fine expression in the mosque of Maryam al-Zamani, fig. 92). Unusual is the elongated rectangle of the courtyard and the additional bazaar forecourt at its eastern end.

The latter two features are taken up again in Shah Jahan's brick and tile Jami^c Masjid at Thatta (1054–68/1644–57).[54] This is otherwise closer to the second type of Shahjahani mosque, since it conforms to the older form of the grid plan as it had been formulated in the Akbari Masjid at Ajmer. The courtyard wings of the Thatta mosque are enriched by a further surrounding aisle.

The Jami^c Masjid of Agra (completed 1058/1648),[55] sponsored by Jahanara, enlarges the plan of the Wazir Khan mosque by doubling the bays of the wings of the prayer-hall. This brings about a deepening of the central *iwan*. The courtyard wings are here formed by continuous arcades interrupted by axial gates.

The scheme is slightly altered in the Jami^c Masjid of Shahjahanabad (1060–66/1650–56; pl. XII), proclaimed as Shah Jahan's counterpart of Akbar's Jami^c Masjid at Fatehpur Sikri,[56] though in fact derived from Jahanara's Agra mosque. The three-bay wings flanking the central domed

142 Delhi, Shahjahanabad, Jami^c Masjid, ground-plan.

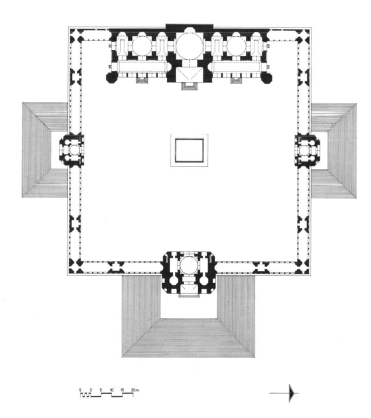

[53] Chaghatai 1975.

[54] Dani 1982, pp. 190–97.

[55] Plan in Chaghatai 1972, fig. 26b.

[56] Koch 1987a, p. 122, and n. 3.

5 0   5   10 15   20m

143 Ajmer, Dargah
of Shaykh Muʿin
al-Din Chishti,
mosque of Shah
Jahan, completed
1046/1636.
(Photo 1978)

144 Ajmer, Dargah,
mosque of Shah
Jahan, ground-plan.

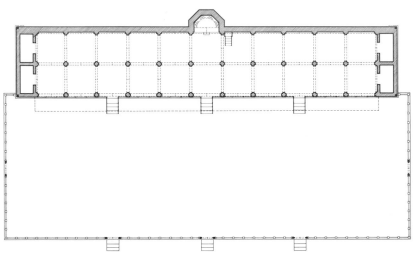

chamber of the prayer-hall are here preceded by two continuous galleries separated by the transverse block of the central *pishtaq*. The front corners of the prayer-hall are accentuated by two high minarets crowned in the typical Mughal fashion by domed *chhatris*.

The type of the massive vaulted prayer-hall continues to appear in smaller mosques, too, often without *sahn*, such as district mosques in the cities (Da'i Anga at Lahore 1045/1635)[57] and funerary mosques; the mosque flanking the Taj Mahall is an abbreviated version of the Jamiʿ Masjid in Agra.

The other main trend of Shahjahani mosques is represented by halls based on the additive system of bays. The bays may have flat or coved ceilings, domes, or even *bangla* vaults. This form, which – as we have seen – relates closely to that of the Diwan-i ʿAmm halls, is preferentially used for smaller marble mosques that express a personal religious commitment of the emperor. Shah Jahan's mosque at Ajmer in the Dargah of Shaykh Muʿin al-Din Chishti was founded in 1628, just before his accession, in fulfilment of

57 Illus. in M. W. U. Khan, p. 45.

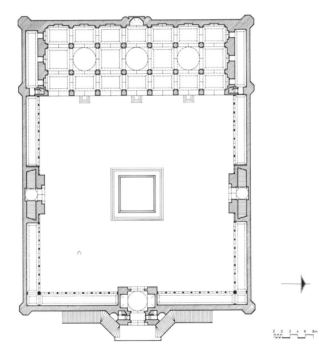

145　Agra fort, Moti
Masjid,
1057–63/1647–53,
prayer-hall, front.
(Photo 1982)

146　Agra fort, Moti
Masjid, ground-plan.

a vow, and completed in 1046/1636. It translates the type of the Patthar Masjid of Srinagar (fig. 91) into a lighter idiom of slender marble pillars, and changes the plan to two aisles of eleven equal bays parallel to the *qibla* wall; all the bays have flat ceilings. New are the two end chambers closing off the shorter sides.

This design culminates in the prayer-hall of the "Moti Masjid" ("Pearl Mosque") in the Agra fort (1057–63/1647–53), integrated in a podium mosque of the *jami* type with a courtyard surrounded by continuous arcaded galleries pierced by three axial gates. The prayer-hall has three aisles parallel to the *qibla* wall, each one of seven bays. All the bays have coved ceilings, with the exception of three domed bays in the central aisle, to which correspond three outer domes. The end rooms of the Ajmer mosque are here joined to a single transversal hall, described as *tanabi khana* in the contemporary texts. Neither the Ajmer mosque nor the Moti Masjid has a central accent in the form of a *pishtaq*.

An abbreviated and miniaturized version of the Ajmer mosque is the "Mina Masjid" ("Gem Mosque") of the Agra palace (completed in 1637), the emperor's private chapel, which has only one aisle of three arcades. Slightly larger and provided with a central feature are two other palace mosques of Shah Jahan. The "Nagina Masjid" ("Jewel Mosque"), completed in 1637, also in the Agra palace, has two aisles of three bays parallel to the *qibla* wall. The

147   Agra fort, Mina Masjid (Shah Jahan's private chapel), 1630s. (Photo 1983)

148   Agra fort, Nagina Masjid, 1630s. (Photo 1978)

two central bays are oblong and covered by *bangla* vaults, the first time this motif appears in Mughal mosque architecture; the new feature is reflected on the facade by a curved-up *bangla* cornice. The "Moti Masjid" in the Lahore fort has two aisles of five bays and a slightly raised central *pishtaq* (fig. 93/7).

A kind of crossbreed between the two main types of Shahjahani mosque architecture is found in the prayer-hall of the small mosque of "Fatehpuri Begam" outside of the western wall of the Taj Mahall complex opposite the tomb of Fatehpuri Begam (fig. 108), probably built by (or for) the same patroness as its larger namesake, the Fatehpuri Masjid at Shahjahanabad (1060/1650). Both have pillared prayer-halls in a particularly delicate idiom of multi-lobed arcades and columns. In front of the *mihrab*, the prayer-halls are transversed by a massive masonry block consisting of a domed chamber preceded by a pronounced *pishtaq*.

Public
buildings

Only scant remains survive of the great metropolitan bazaars, *hammam*s and *sara'i*s of Agra and Shahjahanabad described by the historians of Shah Jahan. Many of these works were conceived in the context of urban planning, which now became a matter of greater concern. A lost bazaar on the plan of a large *muthamman baghdadi* was founded in 1637 at Agra as an organizing link between the Red Fort and the new Jami^c Masjid of Jahanara, which was also projected at this time (fig. 3/9).[58] The space enclosed by the bazaar wings was to serve as a *jilau khana* for the court; the absence of such an assembly-square was now, in a time of greater awareness for ceremony, being criticized as one of the severe shortcomings of the Agra palace. The whole project reflects the preoccupation with urban planning at the time when the concept of Shahjahanabad was beginning to take shape.

In a comparable way, a sequence of bazaars and *karwansara'i*s is used in the Taj Mahall as an articulating element (fig. 108).

[58] Lahori, i/2, pp. 251 f.; ^cInayat Khan, pp. 205 f.

The bazaar in the Red Fort of Shahjahanabad leads in its extension to one of the two principal streets of the city. The building, now called "Chhatta Chauk", is well preserved and still fulfils its purpose. The design of a long vaulted bazaar (*bazar-i musaqqaf*) composed of transverse units set off by pointed transverse arches (figs. 127/2, 130, 131) is unique in India, and stems from Safawid prototypes. Its immediate model, with open *char sus* in the shape of *muthamman baghdadis*, was the no longer extant bazaar at Peshawar constructed by ᶜAli Mardan Khan. Shah Jahan saw and liked it during his Balkh and Badakhshan campaign in 1646. He had its design (*tarh*) sent to Makramat Khan, then chief overseer of the construction of the palace of Shahjahanabad, to be copied.[59]

Nonimperial foundations include the *sara'i* of Amanat Khan (the calligrapher of the Taj Mahall, 1050/1640–41), built next to his tomb, south of Amritsar. It has two gates with remains of good tile mosaic.[60] The "palace" of Aᶜzam Khan at Ahmadabad (1047/1637–38)[61] was, according to its inscription, not only a *sara'i* but also a *qaysariyya* (market); the gate apparently served as a residence for its founder.

The main water-works of Shah Jahan's reign are the canal constructed by ᶜAli Mardan Khan at Lahore[62] and the reactivation of the old canal of Firuz Shah Tughluq, which ran from Khizrabad to Safidun. Under Shah Jahan it was repaired and extended to Shahjahanabad to serve as the main water supply for his new palace and capital.[63]

[59] Kanbo, ii, p. 391.

[60] Begley 1983, pp. 173–78.

[61] Burgess, ii, pp. 58–60, pl. 58.

[62] See above, p. 116.

[63] ᶜInayat Khan, p. 407; Burton-Page 1965a, p. 265.; Gole 1988, p. 25.

Aurangzib (1068–1118/1658–1707)
and Later Mughal Architecture

The success of the architecture created under Shah Jahan may be appreciated from the fact that it affected not only the buildings of his immediate successor Aurangzib but, in the long run, the whole of Indian architecture. Measured against the architectural patronage of his father, that of Aurangzib and his successors has been somewhat underrated and, consequently, very little studied. Aurangzib, however, embarked on a considerable number of architectural enterprises. True to the emperor's orthodox religious convictions, his main interest was directed towards religious architecture and public works.

Palaces and gardens

Neither Aurangzib nor any other of the later Mughals sponsored any major urban palace construction. Aurangzib and his successors did, however, add to the palace-fortresses of Shah Jahan. In 1069–72/1659–62 Aurangzib had the Agra fort surrounded by an additional fortified wall, termed *shir hajji* (figs. 36, 37),[1] undoubtedly to secure the imprisonment of his dethroned father. He also built the ᶜAlamgiri Gate of the fort of Lahore (fig. 93/1).

150 Fatehabad near Agra, garden attributed to Aurangzib, central pavilion. (Photo 1984)

[1] Muhammad Kazim, i, pp. 423–25; Ashraf Husain 1937a, p. 3, n. 1.

[2] The garden is mentioned by Führer 1891, p. 70.

An interesting, so far unpublished garden foundation ascribed to Aurangzib is sited southeast of Fatehabad, southeast of Agra. He is said to have built it after the victory over his brothers in 1659.[2] The garden has the shape of a walled enclosure with towers topped by *chhatris* at its corners. In the centre of the north wall is a gatehouse, to which corresponds an oblong pavilion in the south wall. In the middle of the garden stands a large rectangular pavilion built of brick and red sandstone. It consists of open arcaded aisles set between two closed transversal blocks, each one of three rooms. The pavilion is indebted to ideas of Shahjahani palace architecture; a close parallel is the Rang Mahall in the Red Fort of Delhi (fig. 127/5).

151 Delhi, Red Fort, Zafar Mahall, second third of 19th century and, background right, the Sawan pavilion, completed 1648. (Photo 1981)

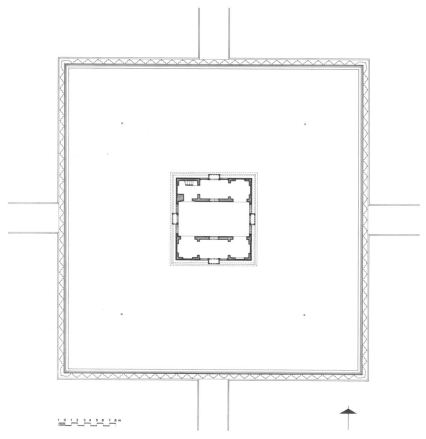

152 Delhi, Red Fort, Zafar Mahall, ground-plan.

One of the main garden foundations of Aurangzib's reign is that of his foster-brother Muzaffar Husayn, entitled Fida'i Khan Koka, at Pinjaur near Chandigarh. It is of the terraced type in the Mughal tradition of Kashmir.[3]

The most important garden palace of Aurangzib's sucessors was the Qud-siyya Bagh at Delhi, built for the mother of the Mughal emperor Ahmad Shah in the 1750s, of which only fragments remain.[4]

[3] Crowe et al., pp. 185–87.

[4] Goetz 1952.

Under the last Mughals the area around the *dargah* of the Chishti saint Qutb al-Din Bakhtiyar Kaki, known as Qutb Sahib, at Mehrauli, Delhi, became the unofficial seat of the emperor. A large ruined palace complex near the *dargah*, the "Zafar Mahall", is said to have been founded by Akbar Shah II (r. 1806–37) and to have been rebuilt by Shah Bahadur II Zafar (r. 1837–58). Its monumental gateway, which bears the date 1264/1847–48, once again revives the time-honoured tradition of facing buildings with red sandstone and white marble at a time when plaster and stucco had become the most widely used material for the rendering of buildings.[5] Other members of the imperial family and the nobility built their *haweli*s, gardens and other secular structures in the same area, much of them having been destroyed or absorbed by later structures.[6] Shah Bahadur II Zafar also constructed a Zafar Mahall in the Red Fort of Delhi in the middle of the pool, which originally formed the centre, of Shah Jahan's fourfold Hayat Bakhsh garden (fig. 127/13). It is a *hasht-bihisht*-inspired pavilion of red sandstone with flat rounded arches and attenuated baluster columns, typical forms of later Mughal architecture and its derivates.[7]

Tombs

The highlight of the sepulchral architecture of Aurangzib is the mausoleum he built for his wife Rabi[c]a Daurani at Aurangabad (1071/1660–61; pl. XVIII). It is a smaller, free copy of the Taj Mahall, not as unsuccessful as usually claimed.[8] Noteworthy is the architectural decoration, in particular the perforated marble screen around the tombstone, the elaborate vaults in *qalib kari* and the wall decoration with *munabbat kari* in polished *chuna*. The patterns continue to feature Shahjahani motifs, but begin to show a certain stiffness. Of high artistic quality is the door in the podium of the tomb, which is covered by *munabbat kari* in embossed brass-sheets showing naturalistic flowery plants surrounded by arabesques (pl. XIX). Similar work appears at about the same time on the gates of the small marble mosque that Aurangzib added to the Red Fort of Shahjahanabad. The door of Rabi[c]a Daurani's tomb bears an inscription giving the date of completion and the name of the architect of the building. It was [c]Ata' Allah, a son of Shah Jahan's architect Ustad Ahmad, who had been especially attached to Aurangzib's arch-enemy, his brother Dara Shukoh.[9] It appears that Aurangzib had to or did not mind to fall back on the architects of the previous reign. The tomb of Rabi[c]a Daurani was to be the last monumental mausoleum of the Mughal dynasty.

Aurangzib's sister Roshanara (d. 1082/1671) is entombed in her garden at Delhi in a flat-roofed *hasht bihisht* pavilion with verandahs of baluster columns and multi-lobed arches. It seems that an already existing garden house was converted into a tomb.[10] Otherwise, the Mughal imperial family reverted with their burials to the example set by the founder of the dynasty, Babur. Neither Jahanara nor Aurangzib allowed any construction over their respective resting-places in Nizamuddin, Delhi (1092/1681)[11] and Khuldabad near Aurangabad. The later Mughals were buried in the Dargah of Qutb Sahib at Merauli,[12] in the Dargah of Nizamuddin[13] or in the tomb of Humayun.[14]

[5] Zafar Hasan 1915–22, iii, p. 50.

[6] Thakur.

[7] Crowe et al., p. 159.

[8] Desai 1974, pp. 313–14, pl. 49.

[9] Chaghatai 1937, p. 206.

[10] Zafar Hasan 1915–22, ii, pp. 266–67.

[11] Zafar Hasan 1922, pp. 16–18.

[12] Zafar Hasan 1915–22, iii, pp. 32 ff.

[13] Zafar Hasan 1922, pp. 18 f.

[14] Naqvi, p. 6.

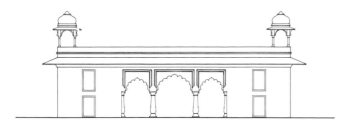

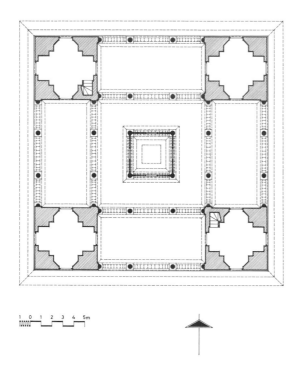

153 *Delhi, tomb of Roshanara, died 1671, ground-plan and elevation.*

The nobility, however, continued to erect sepulchral structures. Still in the classical Mughal spirit is the complex known locally as the Maqbara of ᶜAbd Allah Khan at Ajmer (1114–27/1702–15).[15] It comprises a gate, a mosque and the tombs of ᶜAbd Allah Khan and his wife, all built of white marble. The tomb of ᶜAbd Allah Khan's wife (now cut off by the Beawar Road) is an open tomb enclosure with excellent *jali* screens. The tomb of ᶜAbd Allah Khan was added by his son Sayyid Husayn ᶜAli Khan Barha, one of the two Sayyid brothers who held the real power during the reign of the Mughal emperor Farrukh-Siyar (r. 1712–19). It represents a square *baradari* variant of the hypostyle sepulchral hall with an additional inner domed hall over the tombstone. The multi-lobed arches rest on paired Shahjahani columns, the corners are formed by piers with four half-columns. The style is restrained and retrospective – an unmistakable tribute to Jahangir's and Shah Jahan's marble halls on the bank of the Ana Sagar in the same town (figs. 115, 116).

[15] Tirmizi, pp. 57–61.

[16] See also Andrews 1991b.

[17] Chaghtai 1972.

The tomb of Laʿl Khan at Varanasi (Benares) (1182/1768–69) demonstrates the longlivedness of the Mughal adaptation of the cube-shaped tomb of the Delhi tradition. The design had been introduced into the area with the tomb of Sultan Nithar Begam at Allahabad (fig. 82) which is given here an equally ornate decoration evolved from seventeenth-century Mughal patterns.

Mosques[16]

By far the most impressive building of Aurangzib's reign is the Badshahi Masjid at Lahore (1084/1673–74),[17] the last of the series of the great Mughal *jamiᶜ* mosques in red sandstone (pl. XX). Deviating from the customary local facing with tile-work, it particularly echoes the Jamiᶜ Masjid of Shahjahanabad, but succeeds in conveying a more serene impression by its vast proportions and the quiet juxtaposition of red sandstone with the white marble of its domes and the subtle intarsia decoration. The interior boasts an elaborate decoration of painted plaster relief-work.

The exquisite "Moti Masjid" – Aurangzib's afterthought to the Delhi palace (completed in 1074/1663) – copies Shah Jahan's Nagina Masjid in the Agra fort (fig. 148) almost literally. A new addition is the exuberant floral

156 Lahore, Hazuri Bagh Baradari, built by Ranjit Singh in 1818; behind, the gate of Aurangzib's Badshahi Masjid. (Photo 1980)

decor in marble relief-work, which develops the trend begun under Shah Jahan towards the florid style of later Mughal architecture. The sensuous treatment of the mosque stands in strange contradiction of the unworldly taste professed by its patron – an indication that stylistic developments had begun to become independent from the direct involvement of the Mughal emperor.

Other important foundations of Aurangzib are his mosques at Mathura (1071/1660–61), Benares (1087–88/1676–77) and Lucknow.

The last of the small Mughal mosques faced with white marble is the little-known "Moti Masjid" (1709?) near the Ajmeri Gate of the Dargah of Qutb Sahib at Mehrauli,[18] said to have been sponsored by the Mughal emperor Shah ʿAlam I Bahadur Shah I (r. 1707–12). It departs from the Shahjahani

157 Delhi, madrasa, mosque and tomb of Ghazi al-Din Khan, early 18th century. (Photo 1981)

convention formulated for these marble mosques as pillared halls composed of bays on a grid pattern, and conforms to the other main Mughal mosque type, that of a compact one-aisle prayer-hall, here formed of five bays with a *pishtaq* in the centre.

The *madrasa* and mosque of Ghazi al-Din Khan (d. 1122/1710) at Delhi transposes the scheme of the Khayr al-Manazil of Akbar's reign (figs. 56, 57) into the idiom of the period. Remarkable is the open tomb enclosure of the founder to the south of the mosque, with its floral decor and *jalis* carved of sandstone.[19] The building, which became famous in the nineteenth century as Delhi College, still fulfils its purpose as a Muslim educational institution.

Public works

In the first years of his reign Aurangzib enlarged the Mughal network of roadside accommodation by constructing *sara'i*s equipped with bazaars, mosques, *hammams* and wells, in particular along the roads from Aurangabad to Agra and from Lahore to Kabul. He also ordered the repair of older *sara'i*s and bridges as well as the renovation and refurnishing of mosques in disrepair. The latter works were financed from the emperor's private purse (*sarkar-i khassa sharifa*).[20]

158 Delhi, Red Fort, Moti Masjid, 1663, elevation; the domes were rebuilt after the mutiny of 1857–58. (After Archaeological Survey of India)

[18] Zafar Hasan 1915–22, iii, p. 32.

[19] Zafar Hasan 1915–22, ii, pp. 1–3.

[20] Muhammad Kazim, ii, pp. 1084 f.

SCALE IN METRES

From the late seventeenth century onwards an architectural style developed in India which although derived from Mughal architecture became more and more independent of the Mughal court. The new influential patrons were provincial rulers who proclaimed their defiance of the Mughals by copying their lifestyle and architecture. Typical of this style is a florid ornamental mode with a preference for bulbous shapes, and an increasing use of stucco. The chief elements of this later Mughal fashion were derived from the architectural vocabulary developed in Shah Jahan's reign: columns, pillars, engaged corners shafts and *guldasta*s, all given the characteristic tapering baluster shape with vegetal capital and base (an amazing career for a Dürer column!); multi-lobed arches; bulbous domes; and *bangla* roofs, cornices and vaults, all with sumptuous leaf decoration. These elements were however applied to new architectural contexts, mingled with local styles and used on all types of buildings, minor architecture as well as palaces, fortificatory architecture, mosques, tombs and temples (compare fig. 159 with figs. 134, 135, and fig. 160 with pl. XIII and fig. 121).[1]

159 Govardhan near Mathura, chhatri of Raja Baladeva Singh of Bharatpur (d. 1825), baluster arcades of verandah. (Photo 1978)

160 Jaipur, Hawa Mahall, 1799, facade screen composed of superimposed oriel elements in the shape of domed chhatris and stylized Shahjahani bangla compositions. (Photo 1984)

With regard to building types, Shah Jahan's rooms decorated with mirror mosaic (*ayina kari*) produced particularly numerous offspring; as *shish mahall*s they were employed to give Mughal splendour to the palace of every petty ruler.

By and by the Mughalizing fashion conquered the whole of India. It particularly bloomed under the patronage of the Rajput courts and of the nawwabs of Awadh at Faizabad and Lucknow.[2]

Characteristically, the most outstanding and best preserved example of the late Mughal style at Delhi is the mausoleum of Safdar Jang (1167/1753–54; pl. XXI), the second nawwab of Awadh. It is the last great mausoleum in the classical Mughal tradition of a ninefold plan set on a podium in the centre of a four-parterre *char bagh*.[3]

[1] Burton-Page 1965a, 1971.

[2] Tandon, pp. 66–75.

[3] Zafar Hasan 1915–22, ii, pp. 190–94.

161 Faizabad, tomb of Bahu Begam, c. 1817–56. (Photo 1981)

162 Brighton, Royal Pavilion, 1803–32.

In the eighteenth and nineteenth centuries the influence of the Mughal style extended from the wooden architecture of the Himalayan valleys (Kathmandu, Kulu) to Mysore and Bangalore in Karnataka, and from the Sikh architecture in the Panjab (compare fig. 156 with figs. 151, 153) to Murshidabad and Dacca.[4] Under British patronage the Mughal fashion became a constituent element of the so-called Indo-Saracenic style − the approved idiom of representative buildings.[5] As a typically Indian style it found its way to England in the Indian revivals. The country house Sezincote in Gloucestershire (begun c. 1806), the Royal Pavilion and the Royal Stables at Brighton (1803–32) are the most notable examples.[6]

[4] Goetz 1958.

[5] Metcalf, in particular chs. 3, 4.

[6] Conner, ch. 9.

Of all the architectural styles created under the patronage of the various Muslim dynasties of India, that of the Mughals was the most universal, the most sucessful and the most widely influential. The Mughal style shows the longest continuous development, its after-effects extending well into the twentieth century. In reviewing the whole of Mughal architecture we can discern two main formative phases, that of Akbar and that of Shah Jahan.

In the beginning, the Mughals relied strongly on their already highly developed Timurid architectural heritage, but at the same time they let it enter into a creative dialogue with local building traditions and conditions. The principal trends in the first phase under Babur and Humayun were, on the one hand, imports from Transoxania and broader Khurasan and, on the other hand, the revived ornamental sandstone tradition of the Delhi Sultanate. The two trends were successfully merged in the great architectural synthesis under Akbar, together with other Indian sources that now became equally if not more important. This is particularly true of the architecture of Gujarat and the broader Gujarat-Malwa-Rajasthan tradition.

The first climax of Mughal architecture under Akbar was characterized by a building activity on the grandest scale, not only in the metropolises Agra, Delhi and Lahore, but all over the rapidly expanding empire. The great fortified palace-complexes and the suburban residence Fatehpur Sikri show irregular layouts. That more serious attempts at regular urban planning were not made can be explained by the still strong nomadic heritage of the Mughals, which was not conducive to the foundation of cities. Strict geometrical planning was reserved for the ephemeral architecture of the Mughal camp and for self-contained architectural units such as funerary and residential gardens, *zanana* enclosures, mosques, bazaars and *karwansara'is*. For individual buildings, sepulchral or residential, centralized plans were preferred. Next to the favourite Timurid-derived ninefold plan and its variations, the regular or irregular octagon, the Gujarat-derived plan of a central block, square or rectangular, with an angular ambulatory verandah emerged as the most widely employed model of the period. The cube-shaped domed tomb and the massive one-aisle mosque composed of three or five vaulted bays preserved the Delhi tradition. All plans are thus based on squares, rectangles or octagons. Such plans may also be combined with elevations derived from different sources. On the whole, the logic of the plans is reflected consistently by the elevations.

The rational approach also marks the handling of the architectural decor. Wall decorations are systematized by means of a symmetrical framework, which usually underlines, or at least does not contradict, the tectonics of the building. At the same time, the architectural vocabulary and decoration exhibit a dazzling variety, with the most daring and uninhibited combinations. The unifying material red sandstone mitigates such stylistic clashes very successfully. A closer look reveals a hierarchical or symbolical usage of certain forms. This also applies to the use of colour, white marble being employed to set accents on the prevailing red sandstone.

The main vault types were domes with Timurid arch-netted transition zones, and ribbed domes and ribbed coved ceilings in sandstone taken from the local sandstone styles. At the same time, more complex vaults made their appearance, faced either with decorative stucco shells or with sandstone. Of special interest here is the Khurasan-inspired vault formed by four large ribs crossing each other. The *hammams* as configurations of vaulted units lent themselves particularly well to innovatory work.

In brief, Akbar's architecture can be characterized as a highly dynamic phase which, by syncretizing diverse ingredients, established the basis for all future Mughal architecture.

Under Jahangir followed a more introverted phase of revision, reflection and adaptation. The main concern was to test and further develop selected Akbari solutions rather than to explore new foreign sources. Iranian (Safawid) influence did, however, gain in importance. At times, the architectural designers did not shrink from new solutions, experiments, and even daring extravaganzas.

Sepulchral and residential architecture received particular attention. The tomb types of the previous period were further developed and rendered more complex. The ninefold plan or allusions to it may be integrated into all tomb types, in the substructure of the podium tomb with light superstructures, in the tomb with a central block and ambulatory verandah, and in the cube-shaped tomb. The most typical tomb form of the period is the podium (*takhtgah*) tomb.

Two characteristic Mughal garden forms emerged in this period, the riverside orientated Agra plan and the hillside terraced garden of Kashmir with a central waterway as its main axis. Both plans were to become very influential.

One of the main concerns of the period was the prolific ornamentation of wall surfaces and vaults. A noteworthy feature here is the figurative wall-painting after European models. Local traditions manage to hold their own, as demonstrated by Jahangiri brick architecture faced with tile mosaic at Lahore and in the Panjab.

Vaults now show densely patterned painted stucco shells, in many variations of which the net vault developed from points arranged in concentric tiers was to have a lasting influence. The ribbed coved ceiling of Akbari architecture was transformed into a smooth plastered form equally important for the future.

In this period, broadly speaking, the spadework was done for the following second acme of Mughal architecture under Shah Jahan. Particularly in the last decade of Jahangir's reign a simplified trabeate vocabulary, the increasing use of white marble as facing and for architectural elements and a more sophisticated form of marble intarsia herald the style of Shah Jahan.

Under Shah Jahan Mughal architecture reached maturity and its second climax. The determinant concern was a strict systematization of architecture to conform to the now prevailing ideal of classical equilibrium governed by hierarchical accents. The intensive building activity comprised all domains of architecture. Besides a large number of new foundations, practically all the earlier imperial palace and garden architecture was altered or rebuilt by Shah Jahan. The strict architectural control of even larger spaces became a major concern of the period. The trend resulted in an increased interest in urban planning, which led to the foundation of Shahjahanabad and to the regularization of parts of the cityscape of Agra. The favoured planning principle was that of placing bilateral symmetrical features on either side of a central axis, which was accentuated by a unique feature. Consistent axial planning was now also employed for the large imperial palaces and for the great sepulchral complex of the Taj Mahall. Plans and elevations of individual buildings were generally developed from earlier Mughal designs; the ninefold plan reaches its apogee in the Taj Mahall. Mosques, too, were evolved from earlier types, which were now formally more clearly differentiated according to their function.

However, we also meet with new and foreign types of building such as the great bazaar of the Red Fort of Shahjahanabad, which ultimately goes back to Safawid sources.

The repertory of forms handed down by the architecture of Jahangir was further reduced to a few tried and tested forms, such as the reticulated vault developed from points in concentric circles and the smooth coved ceiling; noteworthy in particular is the concentration on one main columnar form, on one type of bracket and on one type of arch, although their proportions and details may vary. On the other hand, we witness the development of an entirely new vocabulary of architectural forms: curvilinear and — under the inspiration of European models — three-dimensionally modelled, it was to have a lasting influence on Indian architecture. Decoration is more elegant than ever before, thanks to the now favoured use and sophisticated treatment of white marble or highly polished white stucco as facing for imperial buildings. The surfaces may be worked with subtle relief, painting, mirror mosaic and highly refined intarsia in precious *pietre dure*.

With Aurangzib began a process in Mughal architecture which eventually led to its general acceptance as an all-Indian style, not just the expression of a ruling elite. Instrumental for this "Mughalization" of Indian architecture was Shah Jahan's new curvilinear and florid vocabulary, which lent itself well to realization in cheaper, more easily workable materials such as brick rendered with plaster or stucco. Its characteristic forms, the bulbous dome, the *bangla*, multi-lobed arches and baluster-shaped supports, were well suited to giving buildings of any plan, elevation or function the desired Mughal touch, which has up to the present day been associated with imperial splendour and courtly extravagance.

The meaning of vernacular terms has, where possible, been derived from Mughal sources of the sixteenth and seventeenth centuries. Sanskrit-derived terms which were adopted by the Mughals are transliterated according to their spelling by Mughal authors.

ārāmgāh "Place of rest", bedchamber or sleeping-pavilion of the Mughal emperor. Also called **khwābgāh.**

āyīna bandī, āyīna kārī Mosaic of mirror-pieces set in **chūna.**

bāgh Garden.

bakhshī High-ranking Mughal official in charge of military administration and intelligence.

baluster column See **sarw-andām sutūn.**

bangla, bangala Curved-up roof or vault derived from the Bengali hut, hence the name. There are two types of *bangla*, the *do-chala* with a pronounced oblong plan and eaves curved on the longer sides, and the *char-chala* or *chau-chala* with eaves curved on both axes. The term was also applied to pavilions with a *bangla* roof. From the later seventeenth century the term was applied in an even more general way to residential buildings and eventually gave rise to the English word *bungalow.*

bā'ōlī Underground step-well.

bāradarī "Twelve-doored", rectangular or square pavilion with a tripartite arcade or colonnade on each of its sides; more generally, a summer-house.

birka Reservoir, cistern.

burj Tower, usually in a fortificatory context.

chabūtra Raised platform.

chahār bāgh or **chār bāgh** Walled-in garden divided into several compartments. In its canonical Mughal form it has a square plan subdivided into four quarters by paved walkways (**khiyābān**) and canals (**nahr**).

chahār tāq "Four arches", domed structure with four axial arched entrances.

chaitya The horseshoe-arched entrance of the Indian Buddhist temple, usually hewn out of a hillside; miniature forms of the motif also appear as architectural decoration.

chār bāgh See **chahār bāgh.**

chār sū Bazaar crossing. An open square with four arched doorways or gates at the intersection of two bazaar streets or inserted in a single bazaar street; also applied to a bazaar with a **chār sū** crossing.

chatr See **chhatrī**.

chauk Open court, square.

chauk-i jilau khāna. See **jilau khāna**.

chhajjā Sloping or horizontal projection from the top of a wall supported by brackets, to protect from rain or sun.

chhatrī Small (domed) kiosk, usually an open pillared construction; also, a baldachin.

chihil sutūn "Forty-pillared hall", "forty" being used in the sense of "numerous". See also **daulat khāna-i khāṣṣ-o-ᶜāmm**.

chīnī khāna "China room", applied to small wall-niches in which were placed bottles, vases and the like; the motif also appears in relief or inlay work. See also **ṭāqcha**.

chūna, chūnam Highly polished stucco made of powdered marble or shells or of a calciferous white stone quarried in Gujarat that Shah Jahan's writers call *sang-i māhtābī*, *sang-i Pehnālī (Pinhālī?)* or *chūna-i Patiyālī*. Warith (fol. 387ᵛ) describes it as "very white and soft. It can be polished to such a degree that it reflects all things opposite to it like a mirror. In the past this type of plaster coating (*qalᶜi*) was peculiar to [the buildings of] Gujarat. In this . . . reign, which is very active in promoting the arts, it was brought from there in the form of stone by the exalted order [of Shah Jahan] . . . and in due course became common. Most of the imperial buildings have been decorated with marble and mirrorwork (*āyīna kārī*) and all the other [buildings] have been embellished with polished *sang-i Pehnālī*."

commesso di pietre dure The literal translation of this Italian term for Florentine mosaic is "placing together of hard stones"; it refers to a highly specialized form of stone intarsia. Thin slices of stones of extreme hardness (e.g. jasper, chalcedony, agate) are fitted together and fastened in the hollowed-out depressions of the (marble) ground so that the colours and natural marking of the stone form the desired image. Ideally, after the composition of stone pieces has been polished, the joints are not visible in the final design.

coved ceiling Ceiling joined to the wall by a large concave moulding.

coved vault Domical vault whose top is cut with a plane parallel to the floor.

dado The finishing of the lower part of an interior wall from floor to about waist height. Termed **īzāra** by the Mughals.

daftar khāna Office, record-chamber.

dargāh In India, a place or complex where the shrine of a Muslim (Sufi) saint is situated. The Mughals used the term to designate the imperial court.

darwāza Gate, gatehouse, door.

daulat khāna-i khāṣṣ Hall of private audiences. The term was introduced by Shah Jahan. Earlier, this type of ceremonial building had been called *ghusl khāna*.

daulat khāna-i khāṣṣ-o-ᶜamm Hall of public audiences. Since it is a pillared hypostyle construction it is also called **īwān-i khāṣṣ-o-ᶜamm** or **chihil sutūn**.

dīwān Term of various applications, for which see **dīwān-i ᶜamm, dīwān-i khāṣṣ, wazīr**. Also used for the collected works of a poet.

dīwān-i ᶜamm Hall of public audiences.

dīwān-i khāṣṣ Hall of private audiences.

gaz The Mughal linear yard. Also called *zirāᶜ*. The prevailing *gaz* for architecture was the *Gaz-i Ilāhī* introduced under Akbar. Its length was 0.81–0.82 m (See Habib 1963, appendix A).

guldasta "Bunch of flowers", ornamental pinnacle usually terminating in a flower motif, hence the name.

gumbad, gunbad Dome, also used for domed mausoleums.

ḥammām Bath, bath-house; usually consists of a group of rooms for the various stages of the bathing procedure. A Mughal *ḥammām* has three main units, the *rakht kan* (dressing-room), the *sard khāna* (cold room) and the *garam khāna* (hot room).

hasht bihisht "Eight paradises". Building on a ninefold plane. A square or rectangle, often with chamfered corners so as to form an irregular octagon, is divided by four intersecting construction lines into nine parts: a central domed chamber, rectangular open halls in the middle of the sides (in the form of either a **pishṭāq** or a **Mughal īwān**) and double-storey vaulted corner rooms (blocks). There is no hard evidence that this term, which has been coined for Timurid architecture, was actually current in Mughal India.

ḥawelī Building complex for residential use with one or more open courts, often multi-storeyed. The term is used to designate nonimperial residences.

ḥauż Pool, tank.

ḥaẓīra Tomb platform surrounded by a balustraded or latticed screen (Golombek 1969, pp. 100–24).

ḥujra Cell, small room.

ᶜīdgah Open-air place of prayer for Islamic festivals; structure erected there.

īwān A term of various applications, for which see Grabar. Art historians and archaeologists use it to refer to a single vaulted hall walled on three sides and opening directly to the outside on the fourth. For its Mughal use see **Mughal īwān**.

īzāra See **dado**.

jālī Perforated stone screen with ornamental design.

jāmiᶜ masjid Congregational mosque, Friday mosque.

jharōka Architectural frame for official appearances of the Mughal emperor; its conventional shape is that of an overhanging oriel window supported by brackets.

jilau khāna Assembly-place (square) for the retinue of the emperor in front of a palace, a mausoleum or a mosque.

karwānsarāʾī Caravanserai, inn for travellers and merchants and their beasts of burden. Usually a four-sided enclosure with fortified corners and one or two gates; the courtyard may contain a mosque, wells and bazaar streets.

khalwatgāh Retiring-room, private apartment.

khāna Room, house.

khānaqāh Residence for Sufis.

khawāṣṣpūra Quarters for attendants.

khiyābān Paved (raised) walkway, avenue.

khwābgāh "House of dreams", sleeping-pavilion of the Mughal emperor. Also called **ārāmgāh.**

kōs Measure of length equal to about two English miles.

madrasa College of religious education.

maḥall Palace, palace pavilion, apartment, hall; in Mughal India more often applied to the palace quarters of women.

maṇḍal Pavilion, house.

maqbara Burial-palace, graveyard, sepulchre.

marqad Tombstone.

martaba Level, terrace.

masjid Mosque.

mihmān khāna "Guest-house", assembly-hall.

miḥrāb Arched niche in **qibla** wall of a mosque.

miᶜmār Architect.

mīnār (Freestanding) tower.

Mughal īwān Has a special meaning in Mughal architectural terminology, namely a pillared construction of any dimensions and plan. The Mughals derived the term from its Transoxanian use, where it designated the central Asian version of the loggia or verandah with a roof supported by slender wooden columns.

muhandis Geometrician, engineer.

munabbat kārī Relief-work.

muqarnas Concave element in vaults, usually arched, but other forms are also possible. In a dwarf form it may also be used in other architectural contexts, e.g. for capitals of columns.

muthamman baghdādī "Baghdadian octagon", favourite Mughal plan configuration in the shape of a square or rectangle with corners chamfered so as to form an irregular octagon.

nahr Canal; the main canal of a garden (its branch canals may be designated *jadwal* or *jūy*).

nakhsha Plan of a building.

namāzgāh Space for celebration of the major religious festivals.

naqqār khāna, naubat khāna "Drum-house", structure for the court orchestra which accompanied the ceremonial proceedings of the court.

nashīman Pavilion, seat. See also **shāh nashīn**.

naubat khāna See **naqqār khāna**.

parchīn kārī Stone intarsia; also refers to **commesso di pietre dure**.

pietra dura, pietre dure See **commesso di pietre dure**.

pishṭāq High portal, "facade-gateway" (Grabar), usually associated with the **īwān**. In its ripe Mughal form it consists of a monumental arched niche (usually covered by a half-dome) enclosed by a rectangular frame in the shape of an inverted U. Its longer vertical sides are accentuated by engaged polygonal shafts terminating above the parapet in freestanding ornamental pinnacles or **guldasta**s.

pūrṇa ghaṭa Auspicious symbol in Hindu and Buddhist architecture in the form of a pot with overflowing foliage.

qālib kārī "Mould-work", decorative network applied to facing of vaults or cavettos of coved ceilings. The term indicates that in its original plaster form the pattern was applied by means of (wooden?) moulds.

qanāt Subterranean tunnel drawing water from mountain sources by gravity; it has vertical shafts linking it at intervals with the surface.

qarīna Counter-image. Favourite compositional scheme of Shah Jahan's period consisting of two equal features arranged symmetrically on both sides of a central axis.

qayṣāriyya In Safawid Iran a large system of public buildings with covered galleries around an open court. It may contain shops, workshops and also dwellings. The term is also applied to **karwānsarā'i**s.

qibla Direction of Mecca.

qilᶜa Castle, fortress, citadel.

rauża Mausoleum.

ṣaḥn Courtyard.

sarā'ī See **karwānsarā'ī**

sarw-andām sutūn "Cypress-bodied column", baluster column. Column with a tapering shaft forming a bulb at its foot.

Shāhjahānī column Column with a multi-faceted shaft, a multi-faceted or **muqarnas** capital and a base in the form of an inverted cushion capital, whose four flat faces are given a cusped-arch outline that may recall a stylized flower.

shāh nashīn "Royal seat", an arched niche with a half-dome or an alcove of similar shape. Also called **nashīman**.

shīr hajjī Outer fortified wall surrounding a fortress. Kazim (i, p. 424) refers to it as "*faṣil*, which in the language of the common people is called *shīr hajjī*".

shīsh maḥall Room decorated with mirror mosaic (**āyina kārī**).

ṣūfī Islamic mystic.

takhtgāh Platform, podium.

tālār Term of various applications. In Safawid Iran a hypostyle wooden hall with tall columns preceding the vaulted masonry part of a building. Corresponds to the **Mughal īwān**.

ṭambī khāna, ṭanabī khāna Hall or room usually of oblong plan in the interior of a building.

ṭāq Arch.

ṭāqcha Clusters of small decorative wall-niches.

ṭarḥ Design, ground-plan, layout.

verandah Porch or balcony with a roof supported by pillars extending on the outside of a building; a feature of the **Mughal īwān.**

wakīl The highest minister at the Mughal court, but not in charge of a department.

wazīr Minister in charge of imperial finance and revenue collection. Also called *dīwān*.

zanāna Female quarters.

Select Bibliography

Abbreviations
ASIAR Archaeological Survey of India, Annual Report
ASIM Archaeological Survey of India, Memoir
ASIR Archaeological Survey of India, Report
ASINIS Archaeological Survey of India, New Imperial Series
BL British Library
EI² *Encyclopaedia of Islam*, 2nd ed. Leiden: E. J. Brill, 1960–
EIAPS Epigraphia Indica: Arabic and Persian Supplement
IOLR India Office Library and Records

I. Mughal sources

The important position that architecture held in Mughal culture and society is only inadequately reflected in contemporary writing. No special works devoted to architecture have come to light so far, with the exception of the late-seventeenth-century household manual *Bayāż-i Khushbū'ī* (Pers. MS, IOLR Ethé 2784), which contains a section on buildings and gardens. Information has to be distilled from epigraphy, from historiography (architectural descriptions) and from poetry (versified descriptions, eulogies on buildings, and chronogrammes). Much of this material is difficult to obtain as it exists only in manuscript form.

Up to Shah Jahan's reign, Mughal comments on architecture tend to be sparse, vague and unsystematic. An exception is Humayun's author Khwandamir. His descriptions of Humayun's buildings cannot however be verified because they deal with ephemeral architecture and no longer extant buildings. Translations of texts from Akbar's period that deal with architecture have been collected by Brand and Lowry (1985); of particular interest here are the translations from Qandahari. The best source on Jahangiri architecture is Jahangir himself in his memoirs, *Tūzuk*. Information about the architectural patronage of ᶜAbd al-Rahim Khan-i Khanan can be extracted from Nahawandi. Naik also includes discussions of the buildings of the Khan-i Khanan based on contemporary sources.

It was only in Shah Jahan's period that literature was expected faithfully to reflect the building activities of the emperor and to some extent also of the court. This led to architectural descriptions with a consistent terminology, fairly reliable measurements, and occasional observations about style. These descriptions form part of the official histories and may also be incorporated in versified eulogies of buildings. The contemporary texts relating to the Taj Mahall have recently been compiled and translated by Begley and Desai.

From Aurangzib's period onwards the Mughal chronicles are again less explicit about architecture. In the eleventh year of his reign Aurangzib abolished official historiography, the main platform for writing on architecture, supposedly because the sycophantic style of the court historians was not in keeping with his image of a pious ruler. The *Dīwān* of Luṭf Allāh Muhandis contains information about a family of architects who worked under Shah Jahan and Aurangzib (partly trans. by Chaghtai, 1937). An important eighteenth-century source containing information about Mughal architecture from Babur's reign onwards is Shah Nawaz Khan.

ᶜAllāmī, Shaykh Abu'l Faẓl. *Āʾin-i Akbarī.* Pers. text ed. H. Blochmann 2 vols., Calcutta: Royal Asiatic Society of Bengal, 1867—77. Eng. trans. in 3 vols.: i, H. Blochmann, 2nd ed. rev. and ed. D. C. Phillott, 1927; ii and iii, H. S. Jarrett, 2nd. ed. rev. Jadunath Sarkar, 1948—49; rpt. of all 3 vols. New Delhi: Oriental Books Reprint Corporation, 1977—78.

——. *Akbar nāma,* 3 vols. Pers. text ed. Āghā Aḥmad ᶜAlī and ᶜAbd al-Raḥīm, Calcutta: Royal Asiatic Society of Bengal, 1873—86. Eng. trans. H. Beveridge, 1902—39; 2nd rpt. Delhi: Ess Ess Publications, 1979.

Bābur, Ẓahīr al-Dīn Muḥammad. *Bābur nāma,* Eng. trans. A. S. Beveridge, 1921; rpt. New Delhi: Oriental Books Reprint Corporation, 1970.

Badaʾūnī, ᶜAbd al-Qādir. *Muntakhab al-Tawārīkh,* 3 vols. Pers. text. ed. Kabīr al-Dīn Aḥmad, M. A. ᶜAlī and W. N. Lees, Calcutta: Royal Asiatic Society of Bengal, 1864—69. Eng. trans.: i, G. S. A. Ranking; ii, W. H. Lowe; iii, T. W. Haig, 1884—1925; rpt. of all 3 vols. Delhi: Idarah-i-Adabiyat-i-Delli, 1973.

Bukhārī, Khwāja Bahā al-Dīn Ḥasan "Nithārī". *Muzakkir-i aḥbāb* (completed 974/1566), ed. S. M. Fazlullah. Hyderabad: Dāʾirat al-maᶜārif, 1969.

Ḥusaynī, Kāmgār. *Maʾāthir-i Jahāngīrī.* Pers. text. ed. Azra Alavi, Delhi, Aligarh, Bombay: Asia Publishing House Pvt. Ltd., 1978.

Jahāngīr. *Tūzuk.* Pers. text. ed. Sayyid Aḥmad Khān, Aligarh 1864. Eng. trans. Alexander Rogers, ed. Henry Beveridge, 2 vols., 1909—14; rpt. Delhi: Munshiram Manoharlal, 1968.

Kalīm, Abū Ṭālib. *Dīwān.* Pers. text. ed. Partau Bayẓāʾi, Tehran: Khayyam, 1336 sh/1957.

——. *Bādshāh nāma.* Pers. MS. IOLR, Ethé 1570; unpubl. typed transcript, S. M. Yunus Jaffery.

Kanbō, Muḥammad Ṣāliḥ. *ᶜAmal-i Ṣāliḥ,* or *Shāh Jahān nāma,* 3 vols. Rev. Pers. text ed. Waḥid Qurayshī, based on Calcutta ed. (1912—46) by Ghulam Yazdānī, 2nd ed., Lahore: Majlis-i Taraqqī-yi Adab, 1967—72.

Kāẓim, Muḥammad. *ᶜĀlamgīr nāma.* Pers. text. ed. Khādim Ḥusayn and ᶜAbd al-Hayy. Calcutta: Royal Asiatic Society of Bengal, 1865—68.

Khān, ᶜInāyat. *Shāh Jahān Nāma.* Eng. trans. A. R. Fuller, rev. and ed. Wayne E. Begley and Z. A. Desai, New Delhi: Oxford University Press, 1990.

Khān, Muḥammad Bakhtāwar. *Mirʾāt al-ᶜĀlam,* 2 vols. Pers. text. ed. Sājida S. ᶜAlvī, Lahore: Research Society of Pakistan, 1979.

Khān, Muᶜtamad. *Iqbāl nāma-i Jahāngīrī.* Pers. text. ed. ᶜAbd al-Hayy and Aḥmad ᶜAlī, Calcutta: Royal Asiatic Society of Bengal, 1865.

Khān, Shāh Nawāz. *Maʾāthir al-Umarāʾ,* 3 vols. Pers. text ed ᶜAbd al-Raḥīm and Ashraf ᶜAlī, Calcutta: Royal Asiatic Society of Bengal, 1887—96. Eng. trans. Henry Beveridge and Baini Prashad, Calcutta: Asiatic Society, 1911—52; rpt. Patna: Janaki Prakashan, 1979.

Khwāndamīr, Ghiāth al-Dīn. *Qānūn-i Humāyūnī.* Pers. text ed. M. Hidāyat Ḥusayn, Calcutta: Royal Asiatic Society of Bengal, 1940.

Eng. trans. Baini Prashad, Calcutta: Royal Asiatic Society of Bengal, 1940.

Lāhōrī, ʿAbd al-Ḥamīd. *Bādshāh nāma*, 2 vols. Pers. text ed. Kabīr al-Dīn Aḥmad and ʿAbd al-Raḥīm, Calcutta: Royal Asiatic Society of Bengal, 1866–72.

Nahāwandī, ʿAbd al-Bāqī. *Ma'athir-i Raḥīmī*, 3 vols. Pers. text ed. M. Hidāyat Ḥusayn, Calcutta: Royal Asiatic Society of Bengal, 1910–31.

Qandahārī, Muḥammad ʿĀrif. *Ta'rīkh-i Akbarī*. Pers. text ed. S. Muʿin al-Dīn Nadwī, Aźhar ʿAlī Dihlawī and Imtiyāz ʿAlī ʿArshī, Rampur 1382/1962.

Qazwīnī, Muḥammad Amīn, or Amīna-i Qazwīnī. *Bādshāh nāma*. Pers. MS. BL, Or. 173.

Ṭabāṭabā'ī, Jalāl al-Dīn. *Pādshāh nāma*. Pers. MS. BL, Or. 1676.

Wārith, Muḥammad. *Badshāh nāma*. Pers. MS. BL, Add. 6556; unpubl. typed transcript S. M. Yunus Jaffery

Zayn Khān. *Ṭabaqāt-i Bāburī*. Eng. trans. Sayed Hasan Askari, ann. B. P. Ambastha, Delhi: Idarah-i Adabiyat-i Delli, 1982.

II. European sources

From the reign of Akbar onwards the Mughal court was visited by European travellers. Their observations are an indispensable source of information about Mughal architecture. They were able to record their impressions freely, without being subject to the restrictions imposed on the official Mughal historians. However, since as Europeans they had no access to many important buildings, their descriptions are often based not on first-hand knowledge but on hearsay or on texts of other authors.

Bernier, François. *Travels in the Mogul Empire: A. D. 1656–1668.* Eng. trans. Archibald Constable, 1891; rpt. New Delhi: S. Chand & Co. (Pvt.) Ltd., 1972.

Daniell, Thomas and William. Oriental Scenery, London, 1795–1808.

Foster, William, ed. *Early Travels in India: 1583–1619,* 1921; rpt. New Delhi: Oriental Books Reprint Corporation, 1985.

Heber, Bishop Reginald. *Narrative of a Journey through the Upper Provinces of India from Calcutta to Bombay. 1824–25,* 3 vols. London: John Murray, 1828.

Manrique, Fray Sebastien. *Travels of Fray Sebastien Manrique, 1629–1643,* 2 vols. Eng. trans. C. E. Luard and H. Hosten, Oxford: Hakluyt Society, 1927.

Manucci, Niccolao. *Storia do Mogor, or Mogul India: 1653–1708,* 4 vols. Eng. trans. with introduction and notes W. Irvine, 1907; rpt. Calcutta: Editions Indian, 1965–67.

Monserrate, Father Anthony, S. J. *Mongolicae Legationis Commentarius, or The First Jesuit Mission to Akbar.* Latin text ed. Rev. H. Hosten, S. J., in *Memoirs of the Asiatic Society of Bengal,* 3/9 (1914): 513–704. Eng. trans. J. S. Hoyland, annotated S. N. Banerjee, London: Oxford University Press, 1922.

Mundy, Peter. *The Travels of Peter Mundy in Europe and Asia, 1608–1667,* 2 vols. Ed. R. C. Temple, London: Hakluyt Society, 1914.

Pelsaert, Francisco. *A Dutch Chronicle of Mughal India*. Eng. trans. and ed. Brij Narain and Sri Ram Sharma; rpt. Lahore: Sang-e-Meel Publications, 1978.

—. *Jahangir's India*. Eng. trans. W. H. Moreland and P. Geyl, 1925; rpt. Delhi: Idarah-i Adabiyat-i Delli, 1972.

Roe, Sir Thomas. *The Embassy of Sir Thomas Roe to India, 1615–19*. Ed. William Foster, 1899; rpt. rev. ed. London: Oxford University Press, 1926.

Sleeman, W. H. *Rambles and Recollections of an Indian Official*, 1844; rpt. Karachi: Oxford University Press, 1973.

Tavernier, Jean-Baptiste. *Travels in India*, 2 vols. Eng. trans. V. Ball, 2nd. ed. William Crooke, 1925; rpt. New Delhi: Oriental Books Reprint Corporation, 1977.

Thevenot, Jean de. *Voyages: Relation de l'Indoustan, des nouveaux Mogols et des autres peuples et pays des Indes*. Paris 1684. Eng. trans. of pt. 3; *Indian Travels of Thevenot and Careri*, in *India in the Seventeenth Century*, ed. J. P. Guha, New Delhi: Associated Publishing House, 1984.

Andrews, Peter A. 1981. "The Architecture and Gardens of Islamic India". In *The Arts of India*, ed. Basil Gray, Oxford: Phaidon Press, pp. 95–124.

—. 1985. "Trellis Tent and Bulbous Dome". In *Geschichte des Konstruierens i/History of Structural Design i. Konzepte SFB 230/5*: 63–97.

—. 1986a. "Lahawr. Monuments". In EI², v, pp. 559–601, pls. 30, 31.

—. 1986b. "Mahall. vi". In EI², v, pp. 1214–1220.

—. 1987. "The Generous Heart or the Mass of Clouds: The Court Tents of Shah Jahan". *Muqarnas* 4: 149–65.

—. 1991a. "Manzil. In the Eastern Islamic Lands". In EI², vi, pp. 456–457.

—. 1991b. "Masdjid. H. The Architecture of the Mosque. The Monuments: Mughal Empire". In EI², vi, pp. 696–700.

Ansari, M. Azher. 1959. "Palaces and Gardens of the Mughals". *Islamic Culture* 33: 61–72.

Arshi, P. S. 1986. *Sikh Architecture in the Punjab*. New Delhi: Intellectual Publishing House.

Asher, Catherine B. 1981. "The Qalᶜa-i Kuhna Mosque: A Visual Symbol of Royal Aspirations". In CHHAVI 2: *Rai Krishnadasa Felicitation Volume*, Varanasi: Bharat Kala Bhavan, Banaras Hindu University, pp. 212–17.

—. 1984. "The Mughal and Post-Mughal Periods". In *The Islamic Heritage of Bengal*, ed. G. Michell, Paris: UNESCO, pp. 193–212.

Ashraf Husain, M. 1937a. *An Historical Guide to the Agra Fort Based on Contemporary Records*. Delhi: Manager of Publications.

—. 1937b. *A Guide to Fatehpur Sikri*, ed. H. L. Srivastava. Delhi: Manager of Publications.

—. 1965. "Inscriptions of Emperor Babur". EIAPS: 49–66.

III. Secondary Literature

Athar Ali, M. 1985. *The Apparatus of Empire: Awards of Ranks, Offices and Titles to the Mughal Nobility (1574–1658)*. Delhi: Oxford University Press.

Banerji, S. K. 1943. "The Monuments of Aurangzib's Reign". *Journal of the UP Historical Society* 16: 138–47.

Bazmee Ansari, A. S. 1960. "Bustan. Mughal Gardens". In EI², i, pp. 1347–48.

Begley, Wayne E. 1978–79. "Amanat Khan and the Calligraphy on the Taj Mahal". *Kunst des Orients* 12: 5–39.

——. 1979. "The Myth of the Taj Mahal and a New Theory of Its Symbolic Meaning". *The Art Bulletin* 61: 7–37.

——. 1981. "The Symbolic Role of Calligraphy on Three Imperial Mosques of Shah Jahan". In *Kaladarśana: American Studies in the Art of India*, ed. J. Williams. New Delhi: American Institute of Indian Studies, pp. 7–18.

——. 1982. "Ustad Ahmad". In *Macmillan Encyclopedia of Architects*, London: Macmillan, vol. i, pp. 39–42.

——. 1983. "Four Mughal Caravanserais Built during the Reigns of Jahangir and Shah Jahan". *Muqarnas* 1: 167–179.

——. 1985. "A Mughal Caravanserai Built and Inscribed by Amanat Khan, Calligrapher of the Taj Mahal". In *Indian Epigraphy: Its Bearing on the History of Art*, ed. F. M. Asher and G. S. Gai. New Delhi: Oxford & IBH Publishing Co., pp. 283–89.

Begley, Wayne E. and Desai, Z. A. 1989. *Taj Mahal: The Illumined Tomb: An Anthology of Seventeenth-Century Mughal and European Documentary Sources*. Cambridge, Mass.: The Aga Khan Program for Islamic Architecture.

Blake, Stephen P. 1986. "Cityscape of an Imperial Capital: Shahjahanabad in 1739". In *Delhi through the Ages: Essays in Urban History, Culture and Society*, ed. R. E. Frykenberg. Delhi: Oxford University Press, pp. 152–91.

Bloom, Jonathan. 1989. *Minaret: Symbol of Islam. Oxford Studies in Islamic Art 7*.

Bogdanov, L. 1923–24. "The Tomb of the Emperor Babur near Kabul". *Epigraphia Indo-Moslemica:* 1–12.

Brand, Michael and Lowry, Glenn D., eds. 1985. *Fatehpur Sikri: A Sourcebook*. Cambridge, Mass.: The Aga Khan Program for Islamic Architecture at Harvard University and the Massachusetts Institute of Technology.

——. 1987. *Fatehpur Sikri: Selected Papers from the International Symposium on Fatehpur-Sikri Held on October 17–19, 1985, at Harvard University, Cambridge, Massachusetts . . . .* Bombay: Marg Publications.

Brandenburg, Dietrich. 1969. *Der Taj Mahal in Agra*. Berlin: Bruno Hessling.

Brown, Percy. 1942. *Indian Architecture (Islamic Period)*. 7th rpt. of the 1956 ed., Bombay: D. B. Taraporevala Sons & Co. Private Ltd., 1981.

——. 1957. "Monuments of the Mughul Period". In *The Cambridge History of India*, iv, *The Mughul Period*, ed. Wolseley Haig and Richard

Burn. London: Cambridge University Press; 3rd ed. New Delhi:
S. Chand, 1971, pp. 523–76.

Burgess, James. 1900–05. *The Muhammadan Architecture of Ahmadabad,*
2 vols. ASINIS, No. 24. London.

Burton-Page, John. 1960. "Burdj. The Tower in Islamic Architecture in
India". In EI², i, pp. 1321–24.

——. 1965a. "Dihli". In EI², ii, pp. 255–66.

——. 1965b. "Lahore Fort", pp. 82–93; "Wazir Khan's Mosque [Lahore]",
pp. 94–101; "The Red Fort [Delhi]", pp. 130–41; "Fatehpur Sikri",
pp. 142–53; "Taj Mahal [Agra]", pp. 154–65. In *Splendours of the East,*
ed. Mortimer Wheeler. London: Weidenfeld and Nicolson, rpt. Spring
Books, 1970.

——. 1971. "Hind. vii. Architecture. The Mughal Schools". In EI², iii,
pp. 448–52.

——. 1991a. "Makbara. 5. India". In EI², vi, pp. 125–28.

——. 1991b. "Manara. 2. India". In EI², vi.

Carlleyle, A. C. L. 1871–72. "Agra". In ASIR, No. 4, pp. 93–247.

Chagh[a]tai, M. Abdulla[h]. 1937. "A Family of Great Mughal Architects".
Islamic Culture 11: 200–09.

——. 1938. *Le Tadj Mahal d'Agra (Inde): histoire et description.* Brussels:
Editions de la Connaissance.

——. 1941. "Pietra-Dura Decoration of the Taj". *Islamic Culture* 15:
465–72.

——. 1957. *The Description of the Taj Mahal of Agra.* Lahore: Kitab Khana-i
Nauras.

——. 1972. *The Badshahi Masjid: History and Architecture.* Lahore: Kitab
Khana-i Nauras.

——. 1975. *The Wazir Khan Mosque, Lahore: History and Architecture.*
Lahore: Kitab Khana-i Nauras.

——. 1976. *Ta'rikh-i masajid-i Lahaur* ["History of the Mosques of
Lahore", in Urdu]. Lahore: Kitab Khana-i Nauras.

Cole, Major Henry Hardy. 1884. *Preservation of National Monuments,
India: Tomb of Jahangir at Shahdara near Lahore.* Published by Order
of the Governor General in Council for the Office of Curator of
Ancient Monuments in India.

——. 1884. *Preservation of National Monuments, India: Buildings in the
Punjab* [Sarai at Nur Mahal; Plan of Lahore Fort, Shalimar Bagh].
Published by Order of the Governor General in Council for the Office
of Curator of Ancient Monument in India.

Conner, Patrick. 1979. *Oriental Architecture in the West.* London:
Thames & Hudson, chs. 9–11.

de Cosson, A. F. C. 1909. "Chunar". *Bengal: Past and Present* 4 (July-
December): 413–19.

Crane, Howard. 1987. "The Patronage of Zahir al-Din Babur and the
Origins of Mughal Architecture". *Bulletin of the Asia Institute* NS 1:
95–110.

Crowe, Sylvia, Haywood, Sheila and Jellicoe, Susan. 1972. *The Gardens of
Mughal India.* London: Thames & Hudson.

Currie, P. M. 1989. *The Shrine and Cult of Muᶜin al-Din Chishti of Ajmer.* Delhi: Oxford University Press.

Dani, A. H. 1961. *Muslim Architecture in Bengal.* Dacca.

——. 1402/1982. *Thatta: Islamic Architecture.* Islamabad: Institute of Islamic History, Culture and Civilization.

Desai, Z. A. 1961. "Inscriptions from the Khusrau Bagh, Allahabad". EIAPS: 64–68.

——. 1970a. *Indo-Islamic Architecture.* 2nd ed., New Delhi: Publications Division, Ministry of Information and Broadcasting, Government of India, 1986.

——. 1970b. "Some Mughal Inscriptions from Gujarat". EIAPS: 63–92.

——. 1974. "Mughal Architecture in the Deccan". In *History of Medieval Deccan: 1295–1724,* ii (*Mainly Cultural Aspects*), ed. H. K. Sherwani and P. M. Joshi. Hyderabad: The Government of Andhra Pradesh, pp. 305–14.

Desai, Z. A. and Kaul, H. K. 1982. *Taj Museum.* New Delhi: Director General Archaeological Survey of India.

Dickie, James. 1985. "The Mughal Garden: Gateway to Paradise". *Muqarnas* 3: 128–37.

Fergusson, James. 1876. *History of Indian and Eastern Architecture,* rev. and ed. J. Burgess and R. Phene Spiers, London 1910. 2nd Indian rpt. in 2 vols. New Delhi: Munshiram Manoharlal, 1972.

Fischer, Klaus and Christa-M. F. 1976. *Indische Baukunst islamischer Zeit.* Baden-Baden: Holle Verlag.

Freeman-Grenville, G. S. P. 1963. *The Muslim and Christian Calendars, Being Tables for the Conversion of Muslim and Christian Dates from the Hijra to the Year A. D. 2000.* 2nd ed. London: Rex Collings, 1977.

Führer, A. 1889. *The Sharqi Architecture of Jaunpur,* with drawings and architectural descriptions by E. W. Smith, ed. James Burgess. ASINIS, No. 11. Rpt. Varanasi: Indological Book House, 1971.

——. 1891. *The Monumental Antiquities and Inscriptions in the North-Western Provinces and Oudh.* ASINIS, No. 12. Rpt. Varanasi/Delhi: Indological Book House, 1969.

Gascoigne, Bamber. 1971. *The Great Moghuls.* Rpt. London: Jonathan Cape, 1973.

Goetz, Hermann. 1952. "The Qudsia Bagh at Delhi: Key to Late Mughal Architecture". *Islamic Culture* 26/1: 132–51.

——. 1958. "Later Mughal Architecture". *Marg* 11/4: 11–25.

Gole, Susan. 1988. "Three Maps of Shahjahanabad". *South Asian Studies* 4: 13–27.

——. 1989. *Indian Maps and Plans: From the Earliest Times to the Advent of European Surveys.* New Delhi: Manohar.

Golombek, Lisa. 1969. *The Timurid Shrine at Gazur Gah.* Occasional Paper 15, Toronto: Royal Ontario Museum.

——. 1981. "From Tamerlane to the Taj Mahal". In *Islamic Art and Architecture: Essays in Islamic Art and Architecture in Honor of Katharina Otto-Dorn,* i, ed. A. Daneshvari, pp. 43–50.

Golombek, Lisa and Wilber, Donald. 1988. *The Timurid Architecture of Iran and Turan,* 2 vols. Princeton: University Press.

Grabar, O. 1978. "Iwan". In EI², iv, pp. 287–89.

Grover, Satish. 1981. *The Architecture of India: Islamic.* New Delhi: Vikas Publishing House Pvt. Ltd.

Growse, F. S. 1882. *Mathura: A District Memoir.* Rpt. New Delhi: Asian Educational Services, 1979.

Habib, Irfan. 1963. *The Agrarian System of Mughal India (1556–1707).* Bombay: Asia Publishing House.

—. 1987. "The Economic and Social Setting". In *Fatehpur Sikri,* ed. M. Brand and G. D. Lowry. Bombay: Marg Publications, pp. 73–82.

Hambly, Gavin. 1968. *Cities of Mughul India: Delhi, Agra and Fatehpur Sikri.* New York: G. P. Putnam's Sons.

Havell, E. B. 1903. "The Taj and Its Designers". In *The Nineteenth Century and After.* Rpt. in *Essays on Indian Art, Industry & Education.* Madras: G. A. Natesan & Co., 1910, pp. 1–23.

—. 1913. *Indian Architecture: Its Psychology, Structure, and History from the First Muhammadan Invasion to the Present Day.* 2nd ed. London: John Murray, 1927.

Hoag, John D. 1968. "The Tomb of Ulugh Beg and Abdu Razzaq at Ghazni, a Model for the Taj Mahal". *Journal of the Society of Architectural Historians* 27/4: 234–48.

—. 1977. *Islamic Architecture.* New York.

Hodgson, J. A. 1843. "Memoir on the Length of the Illahee Guz, or Imperial Land Measure of Hindostan". *Journal of the Royal Asiatic Society* 7: 42–63.

Hodgson, Marshall G. S. 1974. *The Venture of Islam,* iii: *The Gunpowder Empires.* Chicago/London: University of Chicago Press.

Hosten, Rev. H. 1910. "Who Planned the Taj". *Journal and Proceedings of the Asiatic Society of Bengal* 6: 281–88.

Husain, A. B. M. 1970. *The Manara in Indo-Muslim Architecture.* Dacca: Asiatic Society of Pakistan.

Iizuka, Kiyo. 1969. "Palace Complex of Fathpur Sikri" and "Urban Pattern of Shahjahanabad". *Space Design: Journal of Art and Architecture, Tokyo* 69: 126–74 (in Japanese).

Jain-Neubauer, Jutta. 1981. *The Stepwells of Gujarat in Art-Historical Perspective.* New Delhi: Abhinav Publications.

Jairazbhoy, R. A. 1958. "Early Garden-Palaces of the Mughals". *Oriental Art* NS 4: 68–75.

—. 1961. "The Taj Mahal in the Context of East and West: A Study in the Comparative Method". *Journal of the Warburg and Courtauld Institutes* 24: 59–88.

—. 1972. *An Outline of Islamic Architecture.* Bombay: Asia Publishing House.

Joshi, M. C. 1985. "The Authorship of Purana Qilᶜa and Its Buildings". In *Indian Epigraphy: Its Bearing on the History of Art,* ed. F. M. Asher and G. S. Gai. New Delhi: Oxford & IBH Publishing Co. and American Institute of Indian Studies, pp. 269–74.

Kak, Ram Chandra. 1933. *Ancient Monuments of Kashmir.* Rpt. Sagar Publications, 1971.

Kanwar, H. I. S. 1974. "Ustad Ahmad Lahori". *Islamic Culture* 48: 11–32.

Khan, Ahmad Nabi. 1972. *Maryam Zamani Mosque, Lahore: History and Architecture*. Rpt. from *Pakistan Archaeology* 7 (1972–73), Karachi.

——. 1980a. *The Hiran Minar and Baradari Shaikhupura: A Hunting Resort of the Mughal Emperors*. Lahore: Department of Archaeology and Museums, Ministry of Culture and Tourism, Government of Pakistan.

——. 1980b. "The Tomb of Anarkali at Lahore". *Journal of Central Asia* 3/1: 151–65.

Khan, Iqtidar Alam. 1990. "New Light on the History of Two Early Mughal Monuments of Bayana". *Muqarnas* 6: 55–82.

Khan, M. Wali Ullah. 1961. *Lahore and Its Important Monuments*. 3rd. rev. ed. Lahore: Department of Archaeology and Museums, Ministry of Education, Government of Pakistan.

King, Anthony D. 1984. *The Bungalow*. London.

Klingelhofer, William G. 1988. "The Jahangiri Mahal of the Agra Fort: Expression and Experience in Early Mughal Architecture". *Muqarnas* 5: 153–69.

Koch, Ebba. 1982a. "The Lost Colonnade of Shah Jahan's Bath in the Red Fort of Agra". *The Burlington Magazine* 124/951: 331–39.

——. 1982b. "The Baluster Column – a European Motif in Mughal Architecture and Its Meaning". *Journal of the Warburg and Courtauld Institutes* 45: 251–62.

——. 1983. "Jahangir and the Angels: Recently Discovered Wall Paintings under European Influence in the Fort of Lahore". In *India and the West*, ed. J. Deppert. New Delhi: Manohar, pp. 173–95.

——. 1986a. "Notes on the Painted and Sculptured Decoration of Nur Jahan's Pavilions in the Ram Bagh (Bagh-i Nur Afshan) at Agra". In *Facets of Indian Art: A Symposium Held at the Victoria and Albert Museum on 26, 27, 28 April and 1 May, 1982*, ed. R. Skelton et al. London: Victoria and Albert Museum, pp. 51–65.

——. 1986b. "The Zahara Bagh (Bagh-i Jahanara) at Agra". *Environmental Design*: 30–37.

——. 1987a. "The Architectural Forms [of Fatehpur Sikri]". In *Fatehpur Sikri*, ed. M. Brand and G. D. Lowry. Bombay, Marg Publications, pp. 121–48.

——. 1987b. "Pietre Dure and Other Artistic Contacts between the Court of the Mughals and that of the Medici". In *A Mirror of Princes: The Mughals and the Medici*, ed. Dalu Jones Bombay. Marg Publications, pp. 29–56.

——. 1988a. "[The] Influence [of Gujarat] on Mughal Architecture". In *Ahmadabad*, ed. G. Michell and S. Shah. Bombay: Marg Publications, pp. 168–85.

——. 1988b. *Shah Jahan and Orpheus: The Pietre Dure Decoration and the Programme of Shah Jahan's Throne in the Hall of Public Audiences at the Red Fort of Delhi*. Graz: Akademische Druck- und Verlagsanstalt.

——. 1991a. "The Copies of the Qutb Minar". *Iran*.

——. c. 1991b. "Mughals-Architecture". In EI², vii.

——. c. 1991c. "Muthamman". In EI², vii.

——. (forthcoming). *The Hunting Palaces of Shah Jahan.*

Kuraishi, M. H. 1931. *List of Ancient Monuments Protected under Act vii of 1904 in the Province of Bihar and Orissa.* ASINIS, No. 51. Calcutta: Government of India Central Publication Branch, 1931.

LaRoche, Emmanuel. 1921–22. *Indische Baukunst,* with an introduction by Heinrich Wölfflin and a bibliography by Emil Gratzl. 6 vols. Munich: Bruckmann.

Latif, S. Muhammad. 1892. *Lahore: Architectural Remains.* Rpt. Lahore: Sandhu Printers, 1981.

——. 1896. *Agra: Historical and Descriptive.* Calcutta: Calcutta Central Press.

Lowry, Glenn. D. 1987. "Humayun's Tomb: Form, Function and Meaning in Early Mughal Architecture". *Muqarnas* 4: 133–48.

Luschey-Schmeisser, I. 1969. "Der Wand- und Deckenschmuck eines Safavidischen Palastes in Nayin". *Archaeologische Mitteilungen aus Iran,* NS 2: 183–92.

Metcalf, Thomas R. 1989. *An Imperial Vision: Indian Architecture and Britain's Raj.* London/Boston: Faber & Faber.

Michell, George, ed. 1978. *Architecture of the Islamic World: Its History and Social Meaning.* London: Thames & Hudson.

——, ed. 1984. *The Islamic Heritage of Bengal.* Paris: UNESCO.

Moin-ud-in, Muhammad. 1905. *The History of the Taj and the Buildings in Its Vicinity.* Agra: Moon Press.

Moosvi, Shireen. 1986. "Expenditure on Buildings under Shahjahan – A Chapter of Imperial Financial History". In *Indian History Congress: Proceedings of the Forty-Sixth Session, Guru Nanak Dev University, Amritsar 1985.* Amritsar, pp. 285–99.

Moynihan, Elizabeth B. 1979. *Paradise as a Garden in Persia and Mughal India.* New York: G. Braziller.

——. 1988. "The Lotus Garden: Palace of Zahir al-Din Muhammad Babur". *Muqarnas* 5: 135–52.

Muhammad, K. K. 1986. "The Houses of the Nobility in Mughal India". *Islamic Culture* 60/3: 81–104.

Naik, C. R. 1966. ʿAbduʾr-Rahim Khan-i Khanan and His Literary Circle. Ahmadabad: Gujarat University.

Naqvi, S. A. A. 1946. *Delhi: Humayun's Tomb and Adjacent Buildings.* Delhi: Manager of Publications.

Nath, R. 1970. *Colour Decoration in Mughal Architecture.* Bombay: D. B. Taraporevala Sons & Co. Pvt. Ltd.

——. 1972. *The Immortal Taj Mahal: The Evolution of the Tomb in Mughal Architecture.* Bombay: D. B. Taraporevala.

——. 1976a. *Some Aspects of Mughal Architecture.* New Delhi: Abhinav Publications.

——. 1976b. *History of Decorative Art in Mughal Architecture.* Delhi/Varanasi/Patna: Motilal Banarsidass.

——. 1982. *History of Mughal Architecture,* i [Babur to Humayun]. New Delhi: Abhinav Publications.

——. 1985a. *History of Mughal Architecture*, ii (Akbar A. D. 1556–1605). New Delhi: Abhinav Publications.

——. 1985b. *The Taj Mahal and Its Incarnation: Original Persian Data on its Builders, Material, Costs, Measurements, etc.* Jaipur: The Historical Research Documentation Programme.

——. 1986. *Jharokha: An Illustrated Glossary of Indo-Muslim Architecture.* Jaipur: The Historical Research Documentation Programme.

Nicholls, W. H. 1906–07. "Jahangir's Tomb at Shahdara". ASIAR: 12–14.

——. 1906–07. "Muhammadan Architecture in Kashmir". ASIAR: 161–70.

Nur Bakhsh. 1902–03. "Historical Notes on the Lahore Fort and Its Buildings". ASIAR: 218–224.

——. 1903–04. "The Agra Fort and Its Buildings". ASIAR: 164–193.

O'Kane, Bernard. 1987. *Timurid Architecture in Khurasan.* Costa Mesa: Mazda Publishers.

Pal, Pratapaditya, Leoshko, Janice et al. 1989. *Romance of the Taj Mahal*, exh. cat. Los Angeles/London: Los Angeles County Museum of Art and Thames & Hudson.

Parihar, Subhash. 1985. *Mughal Monuments in the Punjab and Haryana.* New Delhi: Inter-India Publications.

Petruccioli, Attilio and Terranova, Antonio. 1985. "Modelli culturali nell'impianto e nelle trasformazioni di Old Delhi". *Storia della città* 31–32: 123–44.

——. 1988. *Fathpur Sikri: La città del sole e delle acque.* Rome: Carucci Editore.

Pevsner, Nikolaus, Honour, Hugh and Fleming, John. 1966. *The Penguin Dictionary of Architecture.* 3rd. ed. Harmondsworth/Baltimore/Ringwood: Penguin, 1980.

Pougatchenkova, G. A. 1981. *Chefs-d'oeuvre d'architecture de l'Asie Centrale: XIVᵉ–XVᵉ siècle.* Paris: UNESCO.

Qaisar, Ahsan Jan. 1988. *Building Construction in Mughal India: The Evidence from Painting.* Delhi: Oxford University Press.

Rabbani, Ahmad. 1955. "'Haran Munara' at Sheikhupura (Punjab) and Some Problems Connected with It". In *Armughan-i ᶜIlmi: Professor Muhammad Shafiᶜ Presentation Volume*, ed. S. M. Abdullah. Lahore: The Majlis-e-Armughan-e ᶜIlmi, pp. 181–99.

Reuther, Oscar. 1925. *Indische Paläste und Wohnhäuser.* Berlin: Leonhard Preiss Verlag.

Rizvi, S. Athar Abbas and Flynn, Vincent J. A. 1975. *Fathpur-Sikri.* Bombay: D. B. Taraporevala Sons & Co. Pvt. Ltd.

Sanderson, Gordon. 1909–10. "The Diwan-i-ᶜAmm, Lahore Fort". ASIAR: 33–39.

——. 1910–11. "Conservation Work at Agra and Neighbourhood". ASIAR: 94–103.

——. 1911–12. "Shah Jahan's Fort, Delhi". ASIAR: 1–28.

——. 1912–13. "The Nadan Mahall, Solah Khamba, and the Tomb of Ibrahim Chishti, Lucknow". ASIAR: 132–35.

——. 1914. *A Guide to the Buildings and Gardens, Delhi Fort.* 4th ed. Delhi: Manager of Publications, 1937.

Sarda, Har Bilas. 1941. *Ajmer: Historical and Descriptive.* Ajmer: Fine Art Printing Press.

Sharma, Y. D. 1964. *Delhi and Its Neighbourhood.* 2nd ed. New Delhi: Director General, Archaeological Survey of India, 1974.

Shokoohy, Mehrdad and Natalie H. 1988. *Hisar-i Firuza: Sultanate and Early Mughal Architecture in the District of Hisar, India.* London: Monographs on Art, Archaeology and Architecture, South Asian Series.

Siddiqi, W. H. 1972. *Fatehpur Sikri.* New Delhi: Director General, Archaeological Survey of India.

Singh, Chandramani. 1986. "Early 18th-Century Painted City Maps on Cloth". In *Facets of Indian Art*, ed. R. Skelton et al. London: Victoria and Albert Museum, pp. 185–92.

Skelton, Robert. 1972. "A Decorative Motif in Mughal Art". In *Aspects of Indian Art, Papers Presented in a Symposium at the Los Angeles County Museum of Art, October 1970* ed. P. Pal. Leiden: E. J. Brill, pp. 147–52.

Smith, Edmund W. 1894–98. *The Moghul Architecture of Fathpur-Sikri,* 4 vols. ASINIS, No. 18. Rpt. Delhi: Caxton Publications, 1985.

—. 1901. *Moghul Colour Decoration of Agra.* ASINIS, No. 30. Allahabad: Superintendent Government Press, North Western Provinces & Oudh.

—. 1909. *Akbar's Tomb, Sikandarah near Agra, Described and Illustrated.* ASINIS, No. 35. Allahabad: Superintendent Government Press, United Provinces.

Soundara Rajan, K. V. 1983. *Islam Builds in India: Cultural Study of Islamic Architecture.* Delhi: Agam Kala Prakashan.

Tandon, Banmali. 1986. "The Architecture of the Nawabs of Avadh 1722–1856". In *Facets of Indian Art*, ed. R. Skelton et al. London: Victoria and Albert Museum, pp. 66–75.

Thakur, Nalini. 1989. "Mehrauli". In *Architecture and Design 6/1 (Conservation in India)*: 95–104.

Thompson, J. P. 1911. "The Tomb of Emperor Jahangir". *Journal of the Punjab Historical Society* 1: 12–30. Rpt. in *Notes on Punjab and Mughal India,* ed. Z. Ahmed. Lahore: Sang-e-Meel Publications, 1988, pp. 31–49.

Tillotson, G. H. R. 1987. *The Rajput Palaces: The Development of an Architectural Style 1450–1750.* New Haven/London: Yale University Press.

Tirmizi, S. A. I. 1968. *Ajmer through Inscriptions.* New Delhi: Indian Institute of Islamic Studies.

Vats, M. S. 1946. "Repairs to the Taj Mahal". *Ancient India* 1: 4–7.

Villiers Stuart, C. M. 1913. *Gardens of the Great Mughals.* Rpt. Allahabad: R. S. Publishing House, 1979.

Vogel, J. P. 1920. *The Tile-Mosaics of the Lahore Fort.* ASINIS, No. 41. Rpt. Karachi: Pakistan Publications, n. d.

Volwahsen, Andreas. 1969. *Islamisches Indien.* Munich: Hirmer Verlag.

Welch, Anthony and Crane, Howard. 1983. "The Tughluqs: Master Builders of the Delhi Sultanate". *Muqarnas* 1: 123–66.

Wulff, Hans E. 1966. *The Traditional Crafts of Persia: Their Development, Technology, and Influence on Eastern and Western Civilizations.* Cambridge: Massachusetts Institute of Technology.

Yazdani, Ghulam. 1907. "Narnaul and Its Buildings". *Journal of the Asiatic Society of Bengal* NS 3: 581–86 and 639–44.

——. 1929. *Mandu: The City of Joy.* Oxford University Press.

Yaralova, Y. S. 1969. *Arkhitektura stran srednizemnomorya, Afriki i Azii.* Moscow.

Zafar Hasan, M. 1915–22. *Delhi Province: List of Muhammadan and Hindu Monuments,* 4 vols, compiled under supervision of J. F. Blakiston, J. A. Page and Gordon Sanderson. Calcutta, Superintendent Government Printing, India.

——. 1921. *Mosque of Shaikh ʿAbdu-n-Nabi.* ASIM, No. 9. Calcutta: Superintendent Government Printing, India.

——. 1922. *A Guide to Nizamu-d Din.* ASIM, No. 10. Calcutta: Superintendent Government Printing, India.

Index

Numbers in italics indicate figures and plates.